Cambridge
check

Ibukunoluwa
Ogunleye

Updated for 2018

checkpoint
English

3

John Reynolds

Cambridge
checkpoint

Updated for 2018

checkpoint
English

3

HODDER
EDUCATION
AN HACHETTE UK COMPANY

The questions, example answers, and comments that appear in this book were written by the author. In an examination, the way marks would be awarded to answers like these may be different.

Acknowledgements

The author and publishers would like to thank Sue Bonnett for her help during the production of this book.
The publishers would like to thank the following for permission to reproduce copyright material:

Text credits

p.2 Dervla Murphy, 'First, buy your pack animal' from *The Guardian*, 3 January 2009, copyright Guardian News & Media Ltd 2009, reproduced by permission of the publisher; **pp.5–6** Robert Louis Stevenson, extract from *The Amateur Emigrant from the Clyde to Sandy Hook* (1895); **pp.7–9** Michael Palin, extract from *Himalaya* (Weidenfeld & Nicolson, 2004), reproduced by permission of The Orion Publishing Group; **pp.10–11** Charles Dickens, extract from *American Notes* (1842); **p.16** Nelson Mandela, extract from *The Long Walk to Freedom* (Abacus, 1995), copyright © 1994 by Nelson Rolifilala Mandela, reproduced by permission of Little, Brown Book Group and Little, Brown and Company. All rights reserved; **pp.17–18** Minda Magero, extract from 'Memoirs: My primary school experience in Africa' from *http://www.helium.com/items/1011229-memoirs-my-primary-school-experience-in-africa?page=2*, reproduced by permission of Helium Inc.; **pp.19–21** 'The history of Bollywood' from Film 4 website, *http://www.film4.com/features/article/the-history-of-bollywood*; **pp.22–23** 'The ruins of Great Zimbabwe' from *http://www.encounter.co.za/article/81.html*, reproduced by permission of Encounter Magazine; **pp.24–26** Henry Reed, 'Naming of Parts' and 'Judging Distances' from 'Lessons of War' in *Collected Poems, 2/e*, edited by Jon Stallworthy (Carcanet Press, 2007), reproduced by permission of the publisher; **pp.27–29** Laurie Lee, extract from *As I Stepped Out One Midsummer Morning* (Penguin Books, 1971), copyright © Laurie Lee, 1969, reproduced by permission of Penguin Books Ltd. and United Agents on behalf of The Estate of Laurie Lee; **pp.31–32** extract about Benidorm from *http://www.go2benidorm.com*; **pp.32–33** Paul Theroux, extract from *The Pillars of Hercules* (Penguin Books, 2009), copyright © 1995, Cape Cod Scriveners Co, reproduced by permission of the publisher and the Wylie Agency LLC; **p.34** extract on nuclear power from *http://www.greenpeace.org/usa/en/campaigns/nuclear*, reproduced by permission of Greenpeace UK; **pp.34–36** blog by Iris Cheng, 'Chernobyl – distorted reality and unanswered questions', from *http://www.greenpeace.org/international/en/news/Blogs/makingwaves/chernobyl-distorted-reality-and-unanswered-qu/blog/34331*, reproduced by permission of Greenpeace UK; **p.37** overview of nuclear energy from *http://www.world-nuclear.org/education/intro.htm*, reproduced by permission of the World Nuclear Association; **p.40–42** Martin Luther King Jr., extract from 'I have a dream' speech (1963), copyright 1963 Dr Martin Luther King Jr.; copyright renewed 1991 Coretta Scott King, reproduced by arrangement with The Heirs to the Estate of Martin Luther King Jr., c/o Writers House as agent for the proprietor New York, NY; **p.43** extract from information about tigers from *http://www.worldwildlife.org/species/finder/tigers/index.html*, reproduced by permission of WWF; **p.44** extract on Siberian tigers from *http://www.tigersincrisis.com/siberian_tiger.htm*; **p.48** W. B. Yeats, 'The Lake Isle of Innisfree' from *Collected Poems* (Picador, 1990); **pp.49–50** John Betjeman, 'Greenaway' from *Collected Poems* (John Murray, 1972), reproduced by permission of John Murray (Publishers) and Aitken Alexander Associates; **pp.51–52** Anita Desai, extract from 'Games at Twilight' from *Games at Twilight* (William Heinemann, 1978) © 1978 Anita Desai, reproduced by permission of the author c/o Rogers, Coleridge & White Ltd, 20 Powis Mews, London W11 1JN; **pp.53–55** George Orwell, extract from *Down and Out in Paris and London* (Secker & Warburg, 1933), copyright 1933 by George Orwell and renewed 1961 by Sonia Pitt-Rivers, reproduced by permission of Bill Hamilton as the Literary Executor of the Estate of the late Sonia Brownell Orwell and Secker & Warburg Ltd., and Houghton Mifflin Harcourt Publishing Company; **pp.55–57** D. H. Lawrence, 'Snake' from *The Complete Poems of D. H. Lawrence*, edited by V. de Sola Pinto & F. W. Roberts, copyright © 1964, 1971 by Angelo Ravagli and C. M. Weekley, Executors of the Estate of Frieda Lawrence Ravagli. Used by permission of Viking Penguin, a division of Penguin Group (USA) Inc; **pp.58–60** Charles Dickens, extract from *American Notes* (1842); **pp.61–63** William Topaz McGonagall, 'The Tay Bridge Disaster' from *Poetic Gems* (1890); **p.65** Renault Megane advertisement (text and photograph), reproduced by permission of Publicis London; **pp.67–69** 'Why Advertisers Target Children', adapted from *http://kidsandadvertising.co.uk/why-advertisers-target-children.html*, reproduced by permission of KidsandAdvertising; **pp.72–74** Karon Thackston, 'Advertising secrets I learned from the Kirby vacuum cleaner man' from *http://www.businessknowhow.com/marketing/kirbysec.htm*, © 2001 Karon Thackston; **p.78** George Orwell, extract from 'Politics and the English Language' from *Horizon*, Volume 13, Issue 96, April 1946, © George Orwell, 1946 and renewed 1974 by Sonia Orwell, reproduced by permission of Bill Hamilton as the Literary Executor of the Estate of the late Sonia Brownell Orwell and Secker & Warburg Ltd., and Houghton Mifflin Harcourt (published in his volume *Shooting an Elephant and Other Essays*); **pp.79–81** Arthur Conan Doyle, extract from *The Adventures of Sherlock Holmes* (1891–1893); **pp.81–83** Alexander McCall Smith, extract from *Tears of the Giraffe* (Abacus, 2003); **pp.83–85** Susan Hill, extract from *The Woman in Black* (Penguin Books, 1984), © Susan Hill, reproduced by permission of Sheil Land Associates; **pp.86–92** Mark Twain, 'A Ghost Story' from *Sketches New and Old* (1875); **p.104** William Shakespeare, extract from *Romeo and Juliet*.

Photo credits

p.1 © Damian Turski/Alamy; **p.7** © javarman – Fotolia; **p.20** © Ronald Grant Archive; **p.22** © Victor Watts/Rex Features; **p.31** © Lledó – Fotolia; **p.35** © Wendela Hubrecht/Greenpeace; **p.37** © Martin Vonka – Fotolia; **p.40** © Bettmann/CORBIS; **p.44** © Graça Victoria – Fotolia; **p.59** © bedjar – Fotolia; **p.62** © World History Archive/Alamy; **p.67** © Jacek Chabraszewski – Fotolia; **p.80** © Baker Street Scans/Alamy; **p.93** © Kean Collection/Getty Images; **p.97** © Alastair Muir/Rex Features; **p.101** © Tony Larkin/Rex Features; **p.106** © Donald Cooper/Photostage; **p.108** © Juice Images/Alamy

Every effort has been made to trace all copyright holders, but if any have been inadvertently overlooked the publishers will be pleased to make the necessary arrangements at the first opportunity.

Hachette UK's policy is to use papers that are natural, renewable and recyclable products and made from wood grown in well-managed forests and other controlled sources. The logging and manufacturing processes are expected to conform to the environmental regulations of the country of origin.

Orders: please contact Bookpoint Ltd, 130 Milton Park, Abingdon, Oxon OX14 4SB. Telephone: (44) 01235 827720. Fax: (44) 01235 400454. Lines are open 9.00–5.00, Monday to Saturday, with a 24-hour message answering service. Visit our website at www.hoddereducation.com.

© John Reynolds 2011
First published in 2011 by
Hodder Education, an Hachette UK Company,
Carmelite House, 50 Victoria Embankment,
London EC4Y 0DZ

Impression number   11
Year   2019

Cover photo © Michael Filonou/Corbis
Illustrations by Oxford Designers and Illustrators
Typeset in Garamond Light 12pt by DC Graphic Design Limited, Swanley Village, Kent
Printed in India

A catalogue record for this title is available from the British Library

ISBN 978 1444 143874

Contents

Introduction

Welcome to *Cambridge Checkpoint English Student's Book 3*. This is the third of a series of three books aimed at international students in stages 7–9 who are following the Cambridge Lower Secondary curriculum framework for English. Some students may be preparing for the Cambridge Lower Secondary Progression Tests or the Cambridge Lower Secondary Checkpoint Test before going on to Cambridge IGCSE™ English and beyond. This is an integrated series of books (each with an accompanying teacher's resource book), offering a varied and challenging range of English experiences and assignments. The books provide a comprehensive introduction to the skills needed to succeed in English at this stage and can be used as a main teaching resource or to complement teachers' own schemes of work and other materials.

Covering curriculum requirements

The content of *Student's Book 3* is firmly rooted in the Cambridge Lower Secondary English curriculum framework for stage 9 and focuses on the key areas of reading and writing along with underlying emphasis on language study, grammatical usage and punctuation. These skills are consolidated and revisited through each book in the series. Each chapter also contains suggested speaking and listening activities.

In each chapter there is a thematic link between the reading and writing sections, and the stimulus material reflects the suggestions for reading in the Cambridge framework. The stimulus material is drawn from both fiction and non-fiction texts written in English from countries throughout the world and from different periods of time. Pre-twentieth century literature is amply represented and, wherever possible, in an unabridged format. Reading exercises test straightforward fact retrieval, understanding of vocabulary and inferential and interpretative reading skills. Writing tasks allow students to write in a variety of genres (related to the different stimulus material) and provide opportunities to write both short passages and more extended, complex responses, in some cases as part of a small group project.

Structure

Each of the three books comprising the *Cambridge Checkpoint English* series is supported by a teacher's resource book which contains additional reference information, an audio CD and further suggestions for practice exercises related to each chapter in the student's book. A number of pages in the teacher's resource books have been designed for photocopying and use in the classroom.

Each book in the series is divided into eight chapters and follows a similar pattern, beginning with exemplar reading passages illustrating a particular type or genre of writing, followed by exercises to test both understanding and appreciation of what has been read. A range of writing tasks is set, usually linked to the type of writing exemplified by the reading exemplars; there are also suggested speaking and listening activities and, in most chapters, some prose passages or poems intended for general reading interest. Each chapter also contains information on different key skills (punctuation, parts of speech and their functions, vocabulary building and spelling, etc.) and exercises to reinforce these. The final chapter in each book of the series follows a slightly different format from the other seven as it introduces students to a more general area of English study. Although the chapters in each book have been planned so that teachers can work through them progressively in chronological order if they wish, it is not an absolute requirement to approach the course in this way. The books allow for a flexible approach to teaching and the chapters can be taught in whatever order best fits with a teacher's own scheme of work.

Assessment

As mentioned in the previous section, each chapter contains a range of exercises which will allow the assessment of students' progression through the various English skills required for success at this level.

Reading

Travel writing gives accounts of real places in the world in which we live. It is (usually) non-fiction writing and has various forms and purposes. One form is the type of travel writing you will find in guide books or brochures about places that readers may be planning to visit. These publications are concerned mainly with giving information: for example, they may recommend attractions to visit such as museums and zoos; or suggest hotels or campsites in the area; or restaurants that readers might enjoy eating in. You may have come across a similar form of travel writing in newspaper or magazine articles in which journalists review a resort or attraction that they have visited and give their views on its suitability for readers and their families.

However, there is another type of travel writing, in which authors describe in detail a trip they have made. Here the writers include details of people they met during their travels, their impressions of the places they visited (and quite often details of the history of those places) and their thoughts and feelings during their journey. These books may thus be very close to autobiography in their tone and content. In many cases, the authors travelled independently and very often off the usual tourist track. Indeed, some travel writers deliberately draw a distinction between *travellers* (people who travel to places independently, using their own means of transport) and *tourists* (people who visit places as part of their holidays and for whom travel, accommodation and sightseeing visits are arranged for them by a travel company). If we are able or can afford to visit places only as tourists, we may well wish to experience the more exotic parts of the world through reading accounts by travel writers.

The article on pages 2–4 is by Dervla Murphy, an Irish travel writer who has written many books about her experiences while travelling by bicycle or on foot through different countries of the world. As an introduction to the genre of travel writing, read the passage carefully and then answer the questions that follow on page 4.

First, buy your pack animal.

Extract 1: First, buy your pack animal

BY DERVLA MURPHY

In this age of mobile phones, cybercafes and satellite links, it's harder than ever to truly escape ... but not impossible. Dervla Murphy, who has ventured to the ends of the earth with only the most basic provisions, explains how.

The individual traveller's 'age of adventure' has long since been ended by science and technology. Now our planet's few remaining undeveloped expanses are accessible only to well-funded expeditions protected by mobile phones and helicopters – enterprises unattractive to the temperamental descendants of earlier explorers such as Mungo Park and Mary Kingsley. Happily, it's still possible for such individuals to embark on solo journeys through little-known regions where they can imagine how real explorers used to feel.

Reviewers tend to describe my most exhilarating journeys as 'adventures', though to me they are a form of escapism – a concept unfairly tainted with negative connotations. If journeys are designed as alternatives to one's everyday routine, why shouldn't they be escapist? Why not move in time as well as space, and live for a few weeks or months at the slow pace enjoyed by our ancestors? In recent decades everything has become quicker and easier: transport, communications, heating, cooking, cleaning, dressing, shopping, entertaining. However, statistics show increasing numbers of us developing ulcers, having nervous breakdowns, eating too much or too little or retreating from our own reality in plastic-surgery clinics. It's surely time to promote the therapeutic value of slow travel.

There is, of course, a certain irony here: technology has rendered the traditional simple journey somewhat artificial. Previously, those who roamed far and wide had to be isolated for long periods; now isolation is a deliberately chosen luxury. Had I died of a burst appendix in the Hindu Kush or the Simiens or the Andes, it would have been my own fault (no two-way radio) rather than a sad misfortune. Therefore, in one sense, escapist travelling has become a game – but only in one sense. The actual journey is for real: whatever happens, you can't chicken out. You're alone where you've chosen to be, and must take the consequences. (I prefer to forget that nowadays one is never quite alone. With all those satellites, the solitary traveller may be observed picking her nose in the middle of the Great Karoo.)

To facilitate escapism, I offer the following tips ...

1. Choose your country, use guidebooks to identify the areas most frequented by foreigners – and then go in the opposite direction.

It's 'snobbish' to draw a clear distinction between travellers and tourists. Yet it's also realistic. The escapist traveller needs space, solitude, silence. Tragically, during my lifetime, roads have drastically depleted that natural habitat. Adverts for phoney 'adventure tours' make me grind my few remaining teeth. For example, 'England to Kenya by truck! Overland adventure! See five countries in six weeks!' Who in their right mind wants to see five countries in six weeks? How not to escape ... I always try to get off the beaten track. One favourite place where I did so was a trek from Asmara to Addis Ababa. Things are different now, but most people I encountered then had never seen a white person before.

2. Mug up on history.

To travel in ignorance of a region's history leaves you unable to understand the 'why' of anything or anyone. Heavy sociological or political research is unnecessary – although if you happen to fancy that sort of thing it will add an extra dimension to your journey. Learn as much as possible about religious and social taboos, and then scrupulously respect them. Where gifts of money are inappropriate, find out what substitutes to carry. In some countries, a code of conduct towards travellers prevents acceptance of money from guests, so I often buy gifts for the children from the local bazaars.

3. Don't overplan.

At sunrise it's not necessary – nor even desirable – to know where you are going to be at sunset. In sparsely inhabited areas carry a lightweight tent and sleeping bag. Elsewhere, rely on fate to provide shelter: dependence on those met en route greatly enhances escapism, and villagers are unfailingly hospitable to those who trust them. I have been welcomed into villagers' homes everywhere I've cycled or walked, and was always grateful for what was typically a space on the floor. 'Trust' is a key word for relaxed travelling among people whose different way of life may demand adaptability but should prompt no unease or suspicion.

4. Be self-propelling: walk or cycle.

It's important to travel light. At least 75% of the equipment sold nowadays in camping shops – travel clothes lines, rolled-up camping mats, lightweight hairdryers – is superfluous. My primary basics, although it depends on the journey, are a lightweight tent, a sleeping bag suitable for the country's temperature, and a stove. For long treks, far from roads and towns, buy a pack animal to carry food, camping gear, kerosene for your stove if firewood is scarce.

And remember, campsites suitable for you may be disaster areas for a hungry horse or mule. Then you must press on, often to a site hardly fit for humans, but providing adequate grazing. There is nothing more guilt-provoking than seeing a pack animal who has worked hard for you all day denied sustenance.

5. Cyberspace intercourse spoils genuine escapism.

Abandon your mobile phone, laptop, iPod and all such links to family, friends and work colleagues. Concentrate on where you are, deriving your entertainment from immediate stimuli, the tangible world around you. Increasingly, in hostels and guest houses, one sees 'independent' travellers eagerly settling down in front of computers instead of conversing with fellow travellers. They seem only partially 'abroad', unable to cut their links with home.

6. Don't be inhibited by the language barrier.

Although it thwarts exchanges of ideas, it's unimportant on a practical level. I've wandered around four continents using only English and a few courtesy phrases of Tibetan, Amharic, Quechua, Albanian or whatever. Our basic needs – sleeping, eating, drinking – can always be indicated by signs or globally understood noises.

People's features – particularly their eyes – are wonderfully eloquent. In our everyday lives, the extent to which we wordlessly communicate is taken for granted. In 'far-flungery', where nobody within 100 miles [160 km] speaks a word of any European language, one fully appreciates the range of moods and subtle feelings that may be conveyed visually rather than aurally.

7. Be cautious – cautious as distinct from timid.

The assumption that only brave or reckless people undertake solo journeys off the beaten track is without foundation. In fact, escapists are ultra cautious: that's one of their hallmarks, and an essential component of their survival mechanisms. Before departure, they check out likely dangers and either change their route – should these seem excessive – or prepare to deal with any reasonable hazards.

Your outlook on life is also a factor to consider. Why should your bones break abroad rather than at home? Optimists don't believe in disasters until they happen and therefore are not fearful – which is the opposite of being brave.

8. Invest in the best-available maps.

And whatever you do, don't forget your compass.

Guardian

Now answer these questions. Questions 1–5 focus on the first three paragraphs of the article. The remaining questions relate to Dervla Murphy's eight tips for travellers.

Exercise 1: First, buy your pack animal

1 Explain, using your own words, the phrases 'enterprises unattractive to the temperamental descendants of earlier explorers' and 'a concept unfairly tainted with negative connotations'.

2 According to the writer, what have been the effects of science and technology on the experience of travel?

3 Why do you think Dervla Murphy says that slow travel is 'therapeutic'?

4 Explain the 'irony' that Dervla Murphy refers to at the start of paragraph 3 (beginning 'There is, of course, a certain irony here ...').

5 Write a summary of Dervla Murphy's arguments in favour of 'escapist travel' based on the first three paragraphs of her article. You should use your own words and write no more than 120 words.

6 Explain what makes Dervla Murphy annoyed about 'phoney "adventure tours"'.

7 Explain, using your own words, the writer's point about 'trust' at the end of Tip 3.

8 Why might some campsites be 'disaster areas' for a horse or mule?

9 What are the writer's reasons for saying that it is not important to be able to speak the languages of the countries through which you travel?

10 Your cousin and three of his friends are planning to spend six months travelling through some far-off parts of the world before they start university. Write a letter to your cousin in which you give advice for their travels, based on Dervla Murphy's article. You should use your own words.

The advice you have read in Extract 1 is from an experienced modern-day traveller. The next two extracts are accounts of adventurous travels written over 100 years apart.

The first of these passages is by the Scottish author Robert Louis Stevenson (from *The Amateur Emigrant*) and describes his experiences as a passenger in steerage class on a steamer taking emigrants from Scotland to the United States in 1880. Steerage class was the cheapest and least comfortable accommodation on the ship. Read the extract carefully and then answer the questions that follow on page 7.

Extract 2: From the Clyde to Sandy Hook

The wind hauled ahead with a head sea. By ten at night heavy sprays were flying and drumming over the forecastle; the companion [hatch] of Steerage No. 1 had to be closed, and the door of communication through the second cabin thrown open. Either from the convenience of the opportunity, or because we had already a number of acquaintances in that part of the ship, Mr Jones and I paid it a late visit. Steerage No. 1 is shaped like an isosceles triangle, the sides opposite the equal angles bulging outward with the contour of the ship. It is lined with eight pens of sixteen bunks apiece, four bunks below and four above on either side. At night the place is lit with two lanterns, one to each table. As the steamer beat on her way among the rough billows, the light passed through violent phases of change, and was thrown to and fro and up and down with startling swiftness. You were tempted to wonder, as you looked, how so thin a glimmer could control and disperse such solid blackness. When Jones and I entered we found a little company of our acquaintances seated together at the triangular foremost table. A more forlorn party, in more dismal circumstances, it would be hard to imagine. The motion here in the ship's nose was very violent; the uproar of the sea often overpoweringly loud. The yellow flicker of the lantern spun round and round and tossed the shadows in masses. The air was hot, but it struck a chill from its foetor [strong smell].

From all round in the dark bunks, the scarcely human noises of the sick joined into a kind of farmyard chorus. In the midst, these five friends of mine were keeping up what heart they could in company. Singing was their refuge from discomfortable thoughts and sensations. One piped, in feeble tones, 'Oh why left I my hame [home]?' which seemed a pertinent question in the circumstances ...

I now made my bed upon the second cabin floor, where, although I ran the risk of being stepped upon, I had a free current of air, more or less vitiated indeed, and running only from steerage to steerage, but at least not stagnant; and from this couch, as well as the usual sounds of a rough night at sea, the hateful coughing and retching of the sick and the sobs of children, I heard a man run wild with terror beseeching his friend for encouragement. 'The ship's going down!' he cried with a thrill of agony. 'The ship's going down!' he repeated, now in a blank whisper, now with his voice rising towards a sob; and his friend might reassure him, reason with him, joke at him – all was in vain, and the old cry came back, 'The ship's going down!' There was something panicky and catching in the emotion of his tones; and I saw in a clear flash what an involved and hideous tragedy was a disaster to an emigrant ship. If this whole parishful of people came no more to land, into how many houses would the newspaper carry woe, and what a great part of the web of our corporate human life would be rent across for ever!

The next morning when I came on deck I found a new world indeed. The wind was fair; the sun mounted into a cloudless heaven; through great dark-blue seas the ship cut a swath of curded foam. The horizon was dotted all day with companionable sails, and the sun shone pleasantly on the long, heaving deck.

We had many fine-weather diversions to beguile the time. There was a single chess-board and a single pack of cards. Sometimes as many as twenty of us would be playing dominoes for love ... We had a regular daily competition to guess the vessel's progress; and twelve o'clock, when the result was published in the wheel-house, came to be a moment of considerable interest. But the interest was unmixed. Not a bet was laid upon our guesses. From the Clyde to Sandy Hook I never heard a wager offered or taken. We had, besides, romps in plenty. Puss in the Corner, which we had rebaptised, in more manly style, Devil and four Corners, was my own favourite game; but there were many who preferred another, the humour of which was to box a person's ears until he found out who had cuffed him.

This Tuesday morning we were all delighted with the change of weather, and in the highest possible spirits. We got in a cluster like bees, sitting between each other's feet under lee of the deck-houses. Stories and laughter went around. The children climbed about the shrouds. White faces appeared for the first time, and began to take on colour from the wind ... Lastly, down sat the fiddler in our midst and began to discourse his reels, and jigs, and ballads, with now and then a voice or two to take up the air and throw in the interest of human speech.

Robert Louis Stevenson

Exercise 2: From the Clyde to Sandy Hook

1 What does the word 'pens' in paragraph 1 suggest about the state of the accommodation in steerage class? How is this reinforced by the expression 'farmyard chorus' in paragraph 2?

2 Explain, using your own words, what is meant by 'rough billows'.

3 Why does Stevenson describe the song sung in paragraph 2 as containing a 'pertinent question'?

4 From paragraph 4 (beginning 'The next morning when I came on deck ...') choose three descriptive details which convey the change in mood of the weather and conditions on the voyage and say why you have chosen them.

5 By referring to details of Stevenson's account explain as fully as you can the contrast between the earlier and later part of the passage.

6 Choose three expressions from Stevenson's account that suggest that it was written over 100 years ago and give reasons for your choice.

The next extract is by the television presenter and actor Michael Palin and recounts his experiences while making a television programme about his travels through some of the wilder parts of the Himalayas. Here he describes a place called 'Tiger Leaping Gorge', a canyon on the Yangtze River in Yunnan province in south-western China.

Read the passage carefully and then answer the questions that follow.

Extract 3: Tiger Leaping Gorge

Tiger Leaping Gorge

This morning an ethereal mist lingers over the mountains, making breakfast on the terrace a chilly affair. Mr Feng De Fang produces coffee or green tea, walnuts, pancakes with smooth local honey, scrambled egg and fresh apple pie in a crisp batter.

We sit and eat too much and look out over the terraced fields below, where beans, sweetcorn and wheat defy the forces of gravity and an odd mixture of walnut and palm trees cluster around farm buildings whose stone walls are set solid and sturdy against earthquake impact.

It's a serenely calming view, timeless save for a mobile phone inside a doctored mineral-water bottle which hangs out over the balcony on the end of a stick. I ask Mr Feng if they keep it out there for security reasons but he says no, it's the only place they can get reception.

Mr Feng speaks good English, which he says he learnt from British hikers on their way through. Maybe this accounts for the fact that, as we have a group photo taken, he encourages us all with shouts of 'Lovely jubbly!' [a catchphrase from the TV series *Only Fools and Horses*].

The track continues north, clinging to the side of the rock face, the Yangtze a boiling froth 4000 feet [1220 m] below. At one point a sizeable waterfall comes bouncing off the rocks above us and we have to pick our way beneath it, over 50 yards [46 m] of wet stones. I'm most concerned about the horses but they're a lot more sure-footed than I am, perhaps there isn't such a thing as equine vertigo.

The stony, slippery path reaches its narrowest point. The other side of the gorge looms so close that perhaps a tiger might just have made it after all.

Then we're descending fast on steep and potentially lethal tracks of crumbling, chalky rock past bulky rhododendron bushes.

An almost unstoppable momentum delivers us eventually to the river as it emerges from the gorge. It's 100 yards [90 m] wide here and the jade-green stream twists and turns and eddies and swirls between banks of bleached brown boulders. We've been told that a ferry crosses here but it seems highly unlikely. There are no moorings or jetties and the water looks decidedly tricky.

Then I make out some movement on the far bank and a small, steel-hulled boat emerges from beneath the shadow of a colossal overhang and, after taking the current in a wide arc, runs in towards us and docks by ramming its stern hard up between the rocks. Painted lettering on a metal arch at one end of the boat announces it to be the 'Tiger Leaping Gorge Ferry'. We clamber in and a man with a long bamboo pole and the looks and physique of a Spanish gymnast pushes us out onto the Yangtze with a flourish.

The boat seems very fragile all of a sudden. Its two outboard motors do their best but the current seems in control and swings us downstream beneath the overhang, where it's very hot and very quiet. For a moment I'm anxious. The power of the river and the power of the boat seem unfairly matched. The looming rock face above us offers no comfort.

The outboards surge, choke and surge again, but we hold our own against the current and soon we're grinding up onto a gritty beach.

An hour later we've climbed up to where the vehicles are waiting and I look back at the Yangtze, silvery in the twilight and calm and serene now after the trauma of the gorge, and I turn my back on it with a pang of regret.

Michael Palin

Exercise 3: Tiger Leaping Gorge

1 Explain the meaning of the following words and phrases as used in the extract:

ethereal	equine vertigo
serenely	bleached brown boulders
doctored	trauma

2 What do you find surprising about the breakfast produced by Mr Feng De Fang?
3 What do you think the writer means when he says: 'The other side of the gorge looms so close that perhaps a tiger might just have made it after all?'
4 Explain, using your own words, what is meant by 'The power of the river and the power of the boat seem unfairly matched.'
5 Choose two descriptive details used by the writer that suggest the peace and calmness of the area and two which suggest the danger of the journey. Give reasons for your choices.

Exercise 4: Comparing travel writing

By referring to both 'From the Clyde to Sandy Hook'(pages 5–6) and 'Tiger Leaping Gorge'(pages 7–9), explain as fully as you can how each extract does or does not support the principles expressed about travel by Dervla Murphy in 'First, buy your pack animal' (pages 2–4).

Reading for pleasure

In 1842, Charles Dickens and his wife travelled to America. In this passage, he describes his first experience of a 'heavy sea'. Samson was a man famous for his great strength.

American Notes for General Circulation

It is the third morning. I am awakened out of my sleep by a dismal shriek from my wife, who demands to know whether there's any danger. I rouse myself, and look out of bed. The water-jug is plunging and leaping like a lively dolphin; all the smaller articles are afloat, except my shoes, which are stranded on a carpet-bag, high and dry, like a couple of coal-barges. Suddenly I see them spring into the air, and behold the looking-glass, which is nailed to the wall, sticking fast upon the ceiling. At the same time the door entirely disappears, and a new one is opened in the floor. Then I begin to comprehend that the state-room is standing on its head.

Before it is possible to make any arrangement at all compatible with this novel state of things, the ship rights. Before one can say 'Thank Heaven!' she wrongs again. Before one can cry she IS wrong, she seems to have started forward, and to be a creature actually running of its own accord, with broken knees and failing legs, through every variety of hole and pitfall, and stumbling constantly. Before one can so much as wonder, she takes a high leap into the air. Before she has well done that, she takes a deep dive into the water. Before she has gained the surface, she throws a summerset [somersault]. The instant she is on her legs, she rushes backward. And so she goes on staggering, heaving, wrestling, leaping, diving, jumping, pitching, throbbing, rolling, and rocking: and going through all these movements, sometimes by turns, and sometimes altogether: until one feels disposed to roar for mercy.

A steward passes. 'Steward!' 'Sir?' 'What is the matter? What do you call this?' 'Rather a heavy sea on, sir, and a head-wind.'

A head-wind! Imagine a human face upon the vessel's prow, with fifteen thousand Samsons in one bent upon driving her back, and hitting her exactly between the eyes whenever she attempts to advance an inch. Imagine the ship herself, with every pulse and artery of her huge body swollen and bursting under this maltreatment, sworn to go on or die. Imagine the wind howling, the sea roaring, the rain beating: all in furious array against her. Picture the sky both dark and wild, and the clouds, in fearful sympathy with the waves, making another ocean in the air. Add to all this, the clattering on deck and down below; the tread of hurried feet; the loud hoarse shouts of seamen; the gurgling in and out of water through the scuppers; with, every now and then, the striking of a heavy sea upon the planks above, with the deep, dead, heavy sound of thunder heard within a vault; – and there is the head-wind of that January morning.

I say nothing of what may be called the domestic noises of the ship: such as the breaking of glass and crockery, the tumbling down of stewards, the gambols, overhead, of loose casks and truant dozens of bottled porter, and the very remarkable and far from exhilarating sounds raised in their various state-rooms by the seventy passengers who were too ill to get up to breakfast. I say nothing of them: for although I lay listening to this concert for three or four days, I don't think I heard it for more than a quarter of a minute, at the expiration of which term, I lay down again, excessively sea-sick.

Not sea-sick, be it understood, in the ordinary acceptation of the term: I wish I had been: but in a form which I have never seen or heard described, though I have no doubt it is very common. I lay there, all the day long, quite coolly and contentedly; with no sense of weariness, with no desire to get up, or get better, or take the air; with no curiosity, or care, or regret, of any sort or degree, saving that I think I can remember, in this universal indifference, having a kind of lazy joy – of fiendish delight, if anything so lethargic can be dignified with the title – in the fact of my wife being too ill to talk to me ... Nothing would have surprised me. If, in the momentary illumination of any ray of intelligence that may have come upon me in the way of thoughts of Home, a goblin postman, with a scarlet coat and bell, had come into that little kennel before me, broad awake in broad day, and, apologising for being damp through walking in the sea, had handed me a letter directed to myself, in familiar characters, I am certain I should not have felt one atom of astonishment: I should have been perfectly satisfied. If Neptune himself had walked in, with a toasted shark on his trident, I should have looked upon the event as one of the very commonest everyday occurrences.

Charles Dickens

Writing

The most effective travel writing not only successfully creates a vivid sense of place in the reader's mind, but also allows the reader to share in the thoughts and feelings of the writer – it has been said that in the best travel writing you discover as much about the writer as you do about the places he or she has visited. So, much of the enjoyment in reading accounts of travel comes from learning about faraway and exotic places that you may never be able to visit in person. However, a good writer can also make you look differently at places that you know well by writing about them from an unexpected or original point of view. As with any form of writing, close attention to detail and careful choice of descriptive vocabulary are important techniques in bringing the scene to life.

Activities

1 Write an account of a visit to a place that you know well. (It could be somewhere you have gone on holiday or to visit a relative or even the area in which you live.) You should include descriptions of:
- your first impressions on arrival and details of the time of day when you arrived
- the place/s where you stayed and your thoughts about them
- your impressions of some of the local inhabitants
- places of interest which you visited (try to write about at least one which you enjoyed and at least one which you didn't)
- your overall opinion of the place and your thoughts and feelings when you left.

Remember: you know the place well, but you are writing the account for people who have never been there – make sure that you do not leave out important contextual details!

2 Write an account of a journey that you have made that took more than one day. You can describe a journey by any means of transport (on foot, by bicycle, road, rail, sea or aeroplane); the challenge with this task is to make the journey interesting. To do this you need to focus on not just what happened but how the other people involved added to the experience and what your thoughts and feelings were while you were travelling. You can also include details on starting and finishing the journey (for example, by writing about your experiences in the departure and arrival areas of an airport).

Speaking and listening

Paired activity

Working with a friend, each prepare a talk to give to your class. One of you should present arguments in favour of being a traveller and not a tourist, and the other should present arguments in favour of being a tourist and not a traveller. Each of you should try to anticipate and counter the other's arguments. At the end of the presentation, the audience could vote on which talk they found more convincing.

Key skills

Verbs

In *Student's Books 1* and *2*, we looked at the importance of verbs in written and spoken expression. As you will have realised, the verb is one of the most important and complex parts of speech. Here are some more details about verbs and their different functions.

Active and passive voices

English verbs have two **voices**: the **active** and the **passive**. The active voice is when the subject of the verb is responsible for the action of the verb. For example:

The teacher *chose* Sunita to be Form Captain.

In this sentence, the teacher is the subject of the verb *chose* and Sunita is the direct object of this verb. The teacher does the action of the verb so the verb is in the active voice.

However, suppose we turn the sentence round, like this:

Sunita *was chosen* by the teacher to be Form Captain.

Then Sunita, the subject, is not responsible for the action indicated by the verb but has that action done to her – she is said to **suffer** the action of the verb. So here the verb is in the passive voice. In this example of a passive sentence, the teacher (who was the subject of the active sentence in the first example) is known as the **agent**.

Usually, only **transitive** verbs (that is, verbs followed by an object) can be changed from the active to the passive voice because, as you can see in the example above, it is the object of the active verb that becomes the subject of the passive verb.

Infinitives

The infinitives of a verb are nearly always indicated by the word *to*, for example:

to do   to eat   to be

These examples are the **present** infinitive of the **active** form of the verb and are the terms used to describe, or name, these verbs. Here is another example:

The verb *to text* did not exist 30 years ago.

You will also come across forms of infinitive that correspond to the passive voice of a verb, for example:

to be done   to be eaten

These examples are the **present** infinitive of the **passive** form of the verb. (The verb *to be* cannot be used in a passive form.)

There are also different forms of infinitive for the past tense: a **past active** infinitive (e.g. *to have done*) and a **past passive** infinitive (e.g. *to have been done*). Similarly, a **future** infinitive can be formed by using the word *about* (e.g. *about to do* and *about to be done*).

Older books of English usage insist that when an infinitive is used no word should be placed between the *to* and the rest of the infinitive. Breaking this 'rule', as in *to boldly go*, is known as splitting an infinitive. It is better to avoid splitting an infinitive but doing so may produce something that sounds ugly. In this case, it is now usually considered perfectly permissible to use the split infinitive (and it certainly will not be marked as incorrect by examiners!).

Vocabulary

Slang

Slang is informal language, quite often characteristic of a particular group of people (such as teenagers). It is not considered appropriate for formal occasions because it will be understood only by those who are part of the group that uses it. Slang also tends to date very quickly. Although being aware of the latest slang terms is useful when you are talking in English to people of your own age group, it should be avoided when you are writing in any formal way.

Exercise: Slang from the past

Here are some slang terms which were in common use in an earlier period of time. Their meanings are given in the right-hand column but are in the wrong order. Try to match each term with the correct definition.

Slang terms	Definitions
To draw the longbow	Extraordinary
To lay down the knife and fork	To lose courage
To pocket	To go away
To saw your timber	To tell extravagant stories
To get the tail down	To die
Can you dig it?	To have got something right
Bee's knees	To stop talking
To carry a torch for	Do you understand?
To be on the trolley	To put up with
To pipe down	To have a crush on

2 Writing to inform

Reading

In *Student's Books 1* and *2* we looked at ways in which writers give information and learnt about the distinction between facts and opinions. In this chapter and the next, we are going to look at some more-advanced examples of non-fiction writing intended both to give information and to influence the way readers think.

In this chapter, we shall consider some of the ways in which writers give factual information and the different purposes behind their writing. The first two examples are extracts from autobiographies by two African writers: Nelson Mandela and Minda Magero, a poet born in Kenya.

In both of these descriptions, the writers are setting out to **give information** about their lives as children; for example, Nelson Mandela includes a lot of details about the activities that he and his friends engaged in and how they made entertainment for themselves out of what they found around them. Minda Magero gives us information about her first days in school, the way the education system was organised and her personal situation within it, and how the pupils amused themselves. This background information is necessary to enable readers to understand how the experiences of the two writers were influenced by the situations they found themselves in. Both extracts occur at the start of the writers' accounts and so it is important that this factual information is conveyed at this point.

However, although the main focus of these two extracts is to provide some facts, they also contain other details which enrich the accounts. Nelson Mandela talks about the attitude of his people, the Xhosa, towards cattle, as well as reminding us how important it was in this society for boys not to be seen as 'sissies' but to learn the techniques of hunting and fighting. Similarly, Minda Magero describes her emotions and how she was hurt and puzzled by the behaviour of the other girls. At the same time she shows us how now, as an adult, she can understand why they behaved as they did.

Read the first passage carefully and then answer the questions that follow it.

Long Walk to Freedom

From an early age, I spent most of my free time in the veld [largely unforested grassland in Southern Africa] playing and fighting with the other boys of the village. A boy who remained at home tied to his mother's apron strings was regarded as a sissy. At night, I shared my food and blanket with these same boys. I was no more than five when I became a herd-boy looking after sheep and calves in the fields. I discovered the almost mystical attachment that the Xhosa have for cattle, not only as a source of food and wealth, but as a blessing from God and as a source of happiness. It was in the fields that I learned how to knock birds out of the sky with a slingshot, to gather wild honey and fruits and edible roots, to drink warm, sweet milk straight from the udder of a cow, to swim in the clear, cold streams, and to catch fish with twine and sharpened bits of wire. I learned to stick-fight – essential knowledge to any rural African boy – and become adept at its various techniques, parrying blows, feinting in one direction and striking in another, breaking away from an opponent with quick footwork. From these days I date my love of the veld, of open spaces, the simple beauties of nature, the clean line of the horizon.

As boys, we were mostly left to our own devices. We played with toys we made ourselves. We moulded animals and birds out of clay. We made ox-drawn sledges out of tree branches. Nature was our playground. The hills above Qunu were dotted with large smooth rocks which we transformed into our own roller coaster. We sat on flat stones and slid down the face of the large rocks. We did this until our backsides were so sore we could hardly sit down. I learned to ride by sitting atop weaned calves – after being thrown to the ground several times, one got the hang of it.

Nelson Mandela

Exercise 1: Long Walk to Freedom

1 Give the meaning of each of the following words as it is used in the passage:

sissy   mystical   essential   adept   feinting

2 Give three skills that Nelson Mandela learnt during this period of his childhood.

3 Give three things that he particularly enjoyed about these childhood experiences.

4 Write three short paragraphs:
  a) In the first, state all the facts that you have learnt about Nelson Mandela from this passage.
  b) In the second, state all that Nelson Mandela tells you about his thoughts and feelings.
  c) In the third, state all the facts that you have learnt about the countryside in which Nelson Mandela lived in as a child.
  Use your own words as far as possible.

Now read this passage carefully and answer the questions that follow it.

My primary school experience in Africa

My first day at primary school was nothing like my dreams had been. It was January, and I would be turning six that June. Having spent three years in Kindergarten – the third one because I wasn't yet old enough to join primary school – I was rather excited about this new phase of life and learning.

||||➡

In those days, all Kindergarten graduates were assigned to a class or grade called Pre-Primary, where we would earn the right and privilege to join Standard One (First Grade) a year later. My first memory of that day is the sublime pleasure of playing hopscotch in the mid-morning sun with perfect strangers from Pre-Primary. I was just beginning to bond with my playmates when I was suddenly whisked away and deposited in a noisy classroom overflowing with over a hundred First Graders, proud graduates of Pre-Primary. Teachers were assigning students to the three streams that made up First Grade: Red, Yellow or Blue. I glimpsed Dora, a family friend and a familiar face in the crowd, and hurried over to where she was, fervently hoping that we'd be assigned to the same stream. Alas, when our names were called out, I was assigned to 1R and Dora to 1Y!

Joy and laughter turned into bewilderment and sadness later that day as I came face-to-face with another group of perfect strangers: my First Grade classmates. They all knew each other from the year spent together in Pre-Primary, and I immediately became the outsider. Unlike the Pre-Primary crowd, the girls of 1R were vicious and unforgiving: kicking me in the shin and taunting me for I-knew-not-what, while I stood there wondering, 'What have I done?' Years later it would dawn on me that maybe they resented the fact that I had skipped Pre-Primary and gone straight to First Grade. Perhaps the fact that my mother was a teacher at that same school only exacerbated the situation. Throughout my tenure in primary school, my parents made sure that I was a year ahead of my class in learning, a practice that had resulted in my testing out of Pre-Primary and being placed in First Grade.

Minda Magero

Exercise 2: My primary school experience in Africa

1 Give the meaning of each of the following words as it is used in the passage:

   assigned   sublime   fervently   taunting   exacerbated

2 Why did Minda Magero have to spend an extra year in Kindergarten?

3 Explain, using your own words, what happened to Minda on her first day at school (paragraph 2).

4 Give two reasons why the girls in 1R saw Minda as an 'outsider'.

5 Write two paragraphs:
   a) In the first, state all the facts you have learnt about the school Minda Magero attended and the education system of the country in general.
   b) In the second, explain as fully as you can her feelings while she was at school and her thoughts about her school experience now that she is an adult.

Exercise 3: Comparing the extracts

These passages by Nelson Mandela and Minda Magero describe experiences which took place over 50 years apart. What differences and similarities do you find between these two accounts of the writers' early days? You should think about how they describe their experiences, the words and language that they use, as well as the details they give.

Both of the passages are autobiographical and the details we learn from them are primarily about the writers themselves (although we also learn about the country in which they lived as children). In the next two extracts, the character and personality of the writers are unimportant; what these passages are concerned with is conveying information about a particular topic to readers in a direct and objective way.

Read the first passage carefully and then answer the questions that follow on page 21.

The history of Bollywood

Cinema arrived in India on 7 July 1896, when the short films of the Lumière brothers were shown at the Watkins Hotel in downtown Bombay. In 1913, D.G. Phalke, a successful printer, was inspired by seeing *The Life of Christ* on a trip to London. On returning to India, he made the nation's first feature film, *Raja Harishchandra*, based on one of the stories in the religious epic *The Mahabharata*. The film was a huge success. India's film industry has never looked back.

Silent cinema was seized by artists as an opportunity to create a truly international art, one which had none of the language barriers that emerged with the advent of sound. Whereas for the rest of the world it meant cinema could extend beyond national boundaries, for India, with hundreds of languages, silent cinema created an art that reached beyond the nation's many differences.

The flow of the Indian upper classes back and forth between England and India also contributed to a boom in the medium. Producer Himansu Rai and actress Devika Rani returned to India to run one of the first studios together, Bombay Talkies. Rani starred in Rai's first talkie, *Karma* (1933), and went on to become India's first major female star.

In 1931 sound came to Indian cinema with the blockbuster *Alam Ara* (director, Ardeshir Irani), establishing song and dance as part of the story-telling. It also split the film industry along language lines: these broadly being the Hindi belt in the north and the two major language blocks in the south, Tamil and Telegu. But almost each language has its own cinema for those who only understand other dialects such as Kanada or Gujarati etc. Crucially, sound also put a barrier up to the exhibition of Western films. With sound came isolation, and India was able to build up a thriving, distinct indigenous industry to serve its cinema-crazy audience.

Throughout the 1930s the industry operated through a studio system similar to that of Hollywood, with each studio employing its own directors, stars and music directors. The economic boom which followed the coming of sound eventually led to the downfall of this system, as the lucrative business attracted a host of independent producers who quickly

||||➡

set about coaxing the most popular actors and actresses away from the studios that they were contracted to. They did this in the time-honoured fashion of offering them vast sums of cash, the origin of which wasn't always legitimate.

The 1950s were the golden age of Indian cinema. The stars ruled supreme with Dilip Kumar, Dev Anand and Raj Kapoor and their beautiful leading ladies, Nargis, Madhubala, Vyjanthimala and Meena Kumari, becoming gods and goddesses. The great directors who emerged from the studio system, including Raj Kapoor, Mehbood Khan, Guru Dutt and Bimal Roy, produced some stunningly beautiful and powerful films, for example *Devdas* (1955, dir. Bimil Roy), *Pyassa* ('The Thirsty One', 1957, dir. Guru Dutt), *Sri 420* ('Mr 420', 1955, dir. Raj Kapoor), *Kaagaz Ke Phoo* ('Paper Flowers', 1959, dir. Guru Dutt), *Awaara* ('The Rogue', 1951, dir. Raj Kapoor), *CID* (1956, dir. Raj Khosla), all of which only get better with time. The 1940s and 1950s also saw the emergence of the 'playback singer', the off-camera voice that performs the songs that the actors and actresses subsequently mime to. The woman who would dominate the music industry for the next half a century, Lata Mangeshkar, soon to be known as 'the nightingale of India', shot to fame at this time. She was the first playback singer to demand that she should be billed as the singer. She and her younger sister Asha Bhosle sang pretty much every female part for many years. During the 1950s, Mangeshkar recorded four songs a day, and has recorded over 25 000 songs in her long career.

From the 1951 film *Awaara*

Shammi Kapoor exploded onto the screen in the 1961 hit *Junglee* ('The Wild One', dir. Subodh Mukherjee) and the brightly coloured romances really got going. The industry was ruled in the 1960s by 'big banner' production houses which all made highly romantic films. The logical conclusion to this devotion to love, love, love came when Indian girls went nuts over the ultimate chocolate-box hero, the great Rajesh Khanna.

Khanna was subsequently eclipsed by the man who would rule the screen for the next 20 years: Amitabh Bachchan. Although the beginning of his career did not promise superstardom, by 1975 he had become 'the angry young man' and nothing could stop his rise. His fame grew exponentially. When he was seriously injured in 1982, the country came to a standstill. Upon his recovery banners lined the roads declaring, 'God is Great! Amit Lives!'

The 1980s are generally agreed to be the lowest point in the industry's history. Sub-disco music polluted the airwaves and pale imitations of Amitabh Bachchan's angry young man strutted their steroid-enhanced stuff across the screen. The roles for women, which had taken a back seat during the 1970s, became almost non-existent.

A new breed of fresh-faced, happy young men – Aamir Khan, Shah Rukh Khan and Salman Khan (all unrelated) – arrived in the early 1990s. Once again, heroes cared only for getting the girl. These romantic types were the spiritual heirs to their 1960s counterparts. It took just one look and the hero and heroine were transported, usually to Switzerland, to profess their love amongst the mountains. The women made a comeback, with strong actresses such as Manisha Koirala, Madhuri Dixit and now Aishwarya Rai taking bigger roles. Spectacle and 'glamorous realism' continued to be the order of the day. These new stars competed in a radically changed entertainment landscape. The mid-1990s saw cable and satellite arrive in India, opening up more channels for film. The music channels – MTV and Channel V – quickly dropped their Western music and programmed predominantly 'filmi' music videos. As a result a film's music, always important as an advertising hook, took on an even greater importance.

The new millennium has seen the markets and the expectations of Bollywood's traditional audiences change irrevocably; what once worked no longer does. Bollywood's future success depends on whether it can change and adapt to the demands of this new market without losing its core identity; and whether the rest of the world will accept it when it has.

Exercise 4: The history of Bollywood

1 Explain the meaning of the following words as used in the passage:

> advent   blockbuster   indigenous   lucrative
> exponentially   irrevocably

2 The writer of this article also uses some colloquial terms. Explain the meaning of the following:

> went nuts over   ultimate chocolate-box hero
>
> strutted their steroid-enhanced stuff

3 Explain, using your own words, why silent films were originally better suited to the Indian market than talking ones.

4 According to the passage, what has been the main subject of Bollywood films from the 1960s onwards?

5 Write a summary of the development of the Bollywood film industry from 1896 to the present day, using facts taken from the passage. You should write about 250 words and use your own words as far as possible.

6 Although this article is intended to provide factual information, the writer's own views become apparent at times through the language used. Select at least three phrases which convey the writer's own opinions and then explain fully what the opinions are and how the choice of words reveals them.

The next passage gives information about one of the earliest human settlements in Southern Africa. Read it carefully and then answer the questions that follow on page 23.

The ruins of Great Zimbabwe

The complex of ruins known as Great Zimbabwe lies 30 kilometres south-east of Masvingo. It is the symbol modern Zimbabwe took its name from – the word 'Zimbabwe' is derived from the Shona word 'maDzimbabwe', or 'dzimbahwe', meaning 'a great stone building'. Great Zimbabwe is beautifully situated in a fertile and well-watered valley at the head of the Mutirikwi River. Archaeological investigations indicate that this valley, as well as the hill dominating it where the bulk of the ruin stands, were inhabited by several different races from an early age.

Early man sheltered in the caves here, and by the fourth century CE the first Iron Age people, apparently the Gokomere group, found their way to the area and discovered the desirability of the Mutirikwi Valley. It was a place suitable for a king, an oasis of fertility in the wilderness of Africa, with pleasant breezes blowing up the valley to produce a mild and healthy climate.

The hill seems to have attracted the first Iron Age settlers. It was a natural stronghold, easy to defend and dominating the valley.

Over the years so many people settled on the hill that it became overcrowded. Additional building sites were obtained by creating platforms made of piled-up granite rocks forming walls whose insides were filled up with rubble; the conventional African mud-walled huts were then erected on the level surface.

Others settled in the valley at the foot of the hill. It appears that the king, the warriors and the priests of Mwari remained on the hill, while the queen, with the bulk of the people, lived down in the valley. The residence of the king was surrounded by a particularly large, well-built and impressive stone wall.

Considerable archaeological research has not revealed signs of the presence of any people foreign to Africa in these ruins other than a few traders or visitors. The evidence indicates that these vast ruins were built by substantially the same people as those living in Zimbabwe today.

Essentially, the ruins consist of walls made of fragments of granite piled on top of the other. There are two main areas of stone-walled enclosures: in the valley at the foot of the hill, and on the top of the hill.

In the valley at the foot of the hill, more than 900 000 granite fragments were used in the construction of the Imba huru (Great Enclosure). The walls of this impressive structure are decorated with chevron patterns of black and white granite fragments.

The ruins on the hill, the Nharira ya Mambo (Place of the King), originally surrounded the huts of the king, the warriors and the priests.

The builders of the ruins never erected any roofing. Their stonework walls always either enclosed living space, or supported platforms.

The great material wealth of Great Zimbabwe may have been its downfall. After its discovery in the 1870s European adventurers arrived in droves. The rumour started that Zimbabwe was the legendary 'Land of Ophir', the source of King Solomon's gold. The Europeans could not believe that the African 'savages' could build in stone. And so, unfortunately, not much is left of anything since the diggers, looters, and murderers have come and gone.

Yet, there are no ruins like these anywhere else in the world. The small-stone construction gives them immense power in the vast setting of Africa. Large building blocks, curiously, would be dwarfed by the settings, but the cumulative effect of thousands of small, piled fragments is of concentrated human effort.

Exercise 5: The ruins of Great Zimbabwe

Explain as fully as you can what the passage tells us about:
- the location and design of Great Zimbabwe
- the history of the building on the site
- the people who built Great Zimbabwe
- the development and decline of the site
- the writer's opinions about Great Zimbabwe.

You should use your own words as far as possible.

Reading for pleasure

Information is not usually written as poetry. However, in the following pair of poems, the poet Henry Reed uses the situation of being instructed in certain military procedures to make a witty and human response to the purely factual and objective nature of the lessons.

'Naming of Parts'

Today we have naming of parts. Yesterday,
We had daily cleaning. And tomorrow morning,
We shall have what to do after firing. But today,
Today we have naming of parts. Japonica
Glistens like coral in all of the neighbouring gardens,
    And today we have naming of parts.

This is the lower sling swivel. And this
Is the upper sling swivel, whose use you will see,
When you are given your slings. And this is the piling swivel,
Which in your case you have not got. The branches
Hold in the gardens their silent, eloquent gestures,
    Which in our case we have not got.

This is the safety-catch, which is always released
With an easy flick of the thumb. And please do not let me
See anyone using his finger. You can do it quite easy
If you have any strength in your thumb. The blossoms
Are fragile and motionless, never letting anyone see
    Any of them using their finger.

And this you can see is the bolt. The purpose of this
Is to open the breech, as you see. We can slide it
Rapidly backwards and forwards: we call this
Easing the spring. And rapidly backwards and forwards
The early bees are assaulting and fumbling the flowers:
    They call it easing the Spring.

They call it easing the Spring: it is perfectly easy
If you have any strength in your thumb: like the bolt,
And the breech, and the cocking-piece, and the point of balance,
Which in our case we have not got; and the almond-blossom
Silent in all of the gardens and the bees going backwards and forwards,
    For today we have naming of parts.

Henry Reed

'Judging Distances'

Not only how far away, but the way that you say it
Is very important. Perhaps you may never get
The knack of judging a distance, but at least you know
How to report on a landscape: the central sector,
The right of the arc and that, which we had last Tuesday,
    And at least you know

That maps are of time, not place, so far as the army
Happens to be concerned – the reason being,
Is one which need not delay us. Again, you know
There are three kinds of tree, three only, the fir and the poplar,
And those which have bushy tops to; and lastly
    That things only seem to be things.

A barn is not called a barn, to put it more plainly,
Or a field in the distance, where sheep may be safely grazing.
You must never be over-sure. You must say, when reporting:
At five o'clock in the central sector is a dozen
Of what appear to be animals; whatever you do,
    Don't call the bleeders sheep.

I am sure that's quite clear; and suppose, for the sake of example,
The one at the end, asleep, endeavours to tell us
What he sees over there to the west, and how far away,
After first having come to attention. There to the west,
On the fields of summer the sun and the shadows bestow
    Vestments of purple and gold.

The still white dwellings are like a mirage in the heat,
And under the swaying elms a man and a woman
Lie gently together. Which is, perhaps, only to say
That there is a row of houses to the left of the arc,
And that under some poplars a pair of what appear to be humans
    Appear to be loving.

||||➡

Well that, for an answer, is what we rightly call
Moderately satisfactory only, the reason being,
Is that two things have been omitted, and those are very important.
The human beings, now: in what direction are they,
And how far away, would you say? And do not forget
There may be dead ground in between.

There may be dead ground in between; and I may not have got
The knack of judging a distance; I will only venture
A guess that perhaps between me and the apparent lovers,
(Who, incidentally, appear by now to have finished,)
At seven o'clock from the houses, is roughly a distance
Of about one year and a half.

Henry Reed

Writing

If you are writing purely to provide information (for example, giving instructions on how to use a piece of electrical equipment) then it is fully appropriate to use an objective and neutral tone. This is because your readers will be concerned only with the information being given and will not be in any way interested in the person providing that information. However, earlier in this chapter we considered how the writers of two autobiographical extracts (pages 16–18) not only communicated important facts and information about their lives but also expressed this information in such a way that their individual personalities were also conveyed to readers.

One of the key skills in informative writing is striking the correct balance between *what* you are saying and *how* you are saying it in order to engage your readers. Remember this when you attempt the tasks that follow. (On pages 27–29 you will find a further example of autobiographical writing that you may want to use as a model.)

Activities

1 Write about a time when you were involved in an accident or had an illness which prevented you from taking part in everyday activities. (It does not need to be a serious accident or illness.) You should describe how the accident or illness occurred, how you spent your time while you were recovering and what your thoughts and feelings were at the time.

2 Write about a time when you tried to help someone (either a member of your family or a friend) but your actions only made the situation worse. You should describe what the original problem was, what you hoped to do, why things went wrong and what your thoughts and feelings were.

Here is a further autobiographical account that may help you in your writing. It is by Laurie Lee, who, in the late 1930s, set out to walk from his home in England through France to Spain. In this passage he describes parting from his home and family. Note how effectively he conveys his mixed feelings about this experience.

As I Walked Out One Midsummer Morning

The stooping figure of my mother, waist-deep in the grass and caught there like a piece of sheep's wool, was the last I saw of my country home as I left it to discover the world. She stood old and bent at the top of the bank, silently watching me go, one gnarled red hand raised in farewell and blessing, not questioning why I went. At the bend of the road I looked back again and saw the gold light die behind her; then I turned the corner, passed the village school, and closed that part of my life for ever.

It was a bright Sunday morning in early June, the right time to be leaving home. My three sisters and a brother had already gone before me; two other brothers had yet to make up their minds. They were still sleeping that morning, but my mother had got up early and cooked me a heavy breakfast, had stood wordlessly while I ate it, her hand on my chair, and had then helped me pack up my few belongings. There had been no fuss, no appeals, no attempts at advice or persuasion, only a long and searching look. Then, with my bags on my back, I'd gone out into the early sunshine and climbed through the long wet grass to the road.

It was 1934. I was nineteen years old, still soft at the edges, but with a confident belief in good fortune. I carried a small rolled-up tent, a violin in a blanket, a change of clothes, a tin of treacle biscuits, and some cheese. I was excited, vain-glorious, knowing I had far to go; but not, as yet, how far. As I left home that morning and walked away from the sleeping village, it never occurred to me that others had done this before me. ⫴➡

I was propelled, of course, by the traditional forces that had sent many generations along this road – by the small tight valley closing in around one, stifling the breath with its mossy mouth, the cottage walls narrowing like the arms of an iron maiden, the local girls whispering, 'Marry, and settle down.' Months of restless unease, leading to this inevitable moment had been spent wandering about the hills, mournfully whistling, and watching the high open fields stepping away eastwards under gigantic clouds ...

And now I was on my journey, in a pair of thick boots and with a hazel stick in my hand. Naturally, I was going to London, which lay a hundred miles to the east; and it seemed equally obvious that I should go on foot. But first, as I'd never yet seen the sea, I thought I'd walk to the coast and find it. This would add another hundred miles to my journey, going by way of Southampton. But I had all the summer and all time to spend.

That first day alone – and now I was really alone at last – steadily declined in excitement and vigour, as I tramped through the dust towards the Wiltshire Downs a growing reluctance weighed me down. White elder-blossom and dog-roses hung in the hedges, blank as unwritten paper, and the hot empty road – there were few motor cars then – reflected Sunday's waste and indifference. High sulky summer sucked me towards it, and I offered no resistance at all. Through the solitary morning and afternoon I found myself longing for some opposition or rescue, for the sound of hurrying footsteps coming after me and family voices calling me back.

None came. I was free. I was affronted by freedom. The day's silence said, Go where you will. It's all yours. You asked for it. It's up to you now: You're on your own, and nobody's going to stop you. As I walked, I was taunted by echoes of home, by the tinkling sounds of the kitchen, shafts of sun from the windows falling across the familiar furniture, across the bedroom and the bed I had left.

When I judged it to be tea-time I sat on an old stone wall and opened my tin of treacle biscuits. As I ate them I could hear mother banging the kettle on the hob and my brothers rattling their tea-cups. The biscuits tasted sweetly of the honeyed squalor of home – still only a dozen miles away.

I might have turned back then if it hadn't been for my brothers, but I couldn't have borne the look on their faces. So I got off the wall and went on my way. The long evening shadows pointed to folded villages, homing cows, and after-church walkers. I tramped the edge of the road, watching my dusty feet, not stopping again for a couple of hours.

When darkness came, full of moths and beetles, I was too weary to put up the tent. So I lay myself down in the middle of a field and stared up at the brilliant stars. I was oppressed by the velvety emptiness of the world and the swathes of soft grass I lay on. Then the fumes of the night finally put me to sleep – my first night without a roof or bed.

I was woken soon after midnight by drizzling rain on my face, the sky black and the stars all gone. Two cows stood over me, windily sighing, and the wretchedness of that moment haunts me still. I crawled into a ditch and lay awake till dawn, soaking alone in that nameless field. But when the sun rose in the morning the feeling of desolation was over. Birds sang, and the grass steamed warmly. I got up and shook myself, ate a piece of cheese, and turned again to the south.

Laurie Lee

Speaking and listening

Activity

Choose either a sporting fixture that you found particularly exciting or a book, film or television programme that you enjoyed and give an account of what happened in it to your class or small group. You should only include factual details in your talk – do not describe your feelings or your opinions.

Key skills

Verbs

In Chapter 1 we learnt about infinitives. Here is a sentence that includes an infinitive:

I like *to eat*.

In this example, the infinitive form of the verb (*to eat*) functions as the object of the main form of the verb (*like*) and is therefore effectively a noun.

Participles

There are other parts of the verb that also function as different parts of speech. One group is the **participles**, which can function as adjectives. There are both active and passive forms of participle and

	Present participle	Past participle
Active voice	singing	having sung
Passive voice	being sung	having been sung

different participles corresponding to the present and past tenses. The table on the right shows the four participles for the verb *to sing*.

As you can see, the **present participle** in the **active** voice ends in –*ing*. Here is a sentence that uses a present participle in the active voice:

The *singing* bird perched high on the tree.

In this example, the participle *singing* functions as an adjective to describe the bird. Here is similar example:

The audience listened to the choir, *singing* joyfully in the school hall.

This time the present participle introduces an adjectival phrase (or a **participial phrase**) which describes the choir.

The present participle is also very widely used to form different tenses of a verb. In this case it is preceded by some part of the verb *to be* or *to have*. For example:

I *am* singing.

You *will have been* singing this for many years.

When some verbs (like *sing*) form their **past** or **perfect participle** they change a vowel (*sung*); others (like *laugh*) add –*ed* (*laughed*). In the past participle of the **active** voice this part is preceded by *having* (forming *having sung* or *having laughed*). Like present participles, past participles can function as adjectives or adjectival phrases. For example:

Having sung the song, the soloist received a huge round of applause.

The present and past participles in the **passive** voice function in exactly the same way as those in the active voice.

When you are writing, it is important to remember to use the present participle correctly when your participial phrase functions as an adjective. In order to avoid confusing readers, you should ensure that it is always clear exactly which noun a present-participial phrase refers to. Consider the following two sentences and decide which one correctly conveys the meaning the writer intended:

Falling into the water, the lifeguard rushed to save the young child.

The lifeguard rushed to save the young child *falling into the water*.

Misplaced participles are sometimes referred to as **dangling participles**.

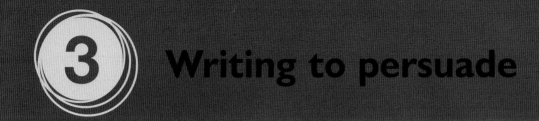

Writing to persuade

Reading

In Chapter 2 we considered writing primarily intended to convey information. Now we are going to look at writing which deliberately aims to persuade readers to think in a certain way. Read carefully the two passages that follow; they both describe the Spanish resort of Benidorm.

Extract 1: Go2benidorm

Benidorm is a Valencia town in the Alicante province of Spain. This coastal town running adjacent to the Mediterranean Sea is a haven for holiday seekers. This is why the population crosses the half-million mark in summer. The festive spirit is reminiscent of the best tourist attractions in the world. The locale is blessed with the giant mountain Puig Campana, which runs through it and adds a lot of freshness conducive to enhancing the tourist spirit.

People who flock to Benidorm feel blessed by the old-world charm of the mountain. After all, is it not the reclusive sylvan spirit which a person seeks during a holiday? Benidorm is the right mix of the ancient with the current; the mountains with the skyscrapers.

The top tourist attractions in Benidorm are the three beaches that line its arena. These are the Llevant, Ponent and Mal Pas. These are all recognised with a blue flag, which is the highest grade provided by the European Union. The beaches are dotted with skyscrapers and a Spanish beach culture. The aroma of food and soft carnival music waft in the air. There is not a thing you can't enjoy at the beaches if you are ready to join the festive spirit. ▐▐▐➤

Wednesday and Sunday are marketplace days. They offer a lot of what the eyes won't ever get tired of seeing. There are avenues, lanes, bazaars, all laid out with goods of all kinds. In the dust and haze created, the sale bazaar reminds us of the barter sales of thousands of years ago, when the world was still untouched by vanity, pilferage and the need to outdo others. There are leather goods, glassware, tablecloths, shoes and practically anything that's a profitable import or that is made by the local craftsmen. The idea is to bargain and bargain well.

The great attraction of Benidorm is its no-holds-barred cosmopolitan touch and the fact that it caters equally for all age groups. Don't miss the call of the Mediterranean. It provides a perfect place to relax and escape from the mundane existence of everyday life.

Extract 2: Benidorm in winter

Benidorm was a mass of beachside high-rises, the worst place I had seen on the coast so far, worse than Torremolinos, which was slap-happy seaside tackiness of a familiar and forgivable kind. But Benidorm was ugliness on a grand scale — tall blocks of apartments, hideous hotels, winking signs, the whole place was badly built and visually unappealing. Everything that Spain was said to stand for — charm, dignity, elegance, honour, restraint — was denied in the look of Benidorm. And because this was wet chilly winter, the wide streets were empty, most of the hotels were shut, no one sat on the beach or swam in the sea: the useless horror, naked and raw in the low season, was demoralising and awful.

In 1949, Benidorm was a tiny impoverished fishing village, 'said to be an open door for smugglers', an English visitor wrote. I walked around. I had a pizza. I sat on a bench surveying the Mediterranean, and then the wind picked up and the rain began.

The rain delighted me. It whipped against the sea. It darkened the stone of the hotels and tore at the signs. It coursed down the empty streets and flooded the gutters and cut gullies through the beach sand. A bit more wind and the lights would fail, a bit more rain and it would be a real flood. And that would be the answer, the cure for Benidorm – nature's revenge, an elemental purifying storm that would wipe the place out.

It lifted my spirits to imagine the destruction of such a place, and I boarded the onward train feeling joy in my heart at the prospect of the wholesale destruction. The rain swept loudly against the side of the railway car like a shower of gravel.

Paul Theroux
(from his book The Pillars of Hercules)

Extract 1 is clearly aimed at attracting people to visit Benidorm. Extract 2 is by the travel writer Paul Theroux and presents a completely different picture of the town. Exercise 1 on page 34 asks you to compare these extracts but its purpose is not to argue over which of these views is the 'right' one. Your task is to consider how the content and language of each passage succeeds in persuading readers to share the opinions of the writer.

For example, Extract 1 focuses on the positive aspects of the town. Although it insists that Benidorm is perfectly suited to all the requirements of the modern holidaymaker, it places great emphasis on the old-world charm of the surrounding countryside and the way in which the marketplace recalls earlier (and more innocent) times. Another factor in this description is, not surprisingly, the emphasis on the summer attractions of the town – the sun, the sandy beaches and the range of tourist attractions. Expressions such as 'reclusive sylvan spirit' reinforce the sense of old-world charm ('sylvan', in particular, suggests idealistic country scenes of ancient times). Conversely, the passage mentions that the beaches are 'dotted' with skyscrapers (implying that they are few and far between) and that the town appeals to a 'cosmopolitan' group of people, suggesting somewhere sophisticated.

Paul Theroux is clearly unimpressed with Benidorm and communicates his feelings forcefully to his readers. In contrast to Extract 1, he describes the town in winter when it is empty and in particularly wet and unpleasant weather conditions. His reference to the town's past history describes it as a 'tiny impoverished fishing village' that was the haunt of smugglers, suggesting it had a sordid and unattractive past. He reinforces this by his uncompromising statements about its 'ugliness' and references to the 'tall blocks of apartments, hideous hotels' which appear to be more than just dotted along the seashore.

It is unlikely that either description gives an accurate representation of the town but each writer is successful in presenting their intended image of Benidorm.

Exercise 1: Comparing Extracts 1 and 2

Write a comparison of the two descriptions of Benidorm and say which you find the more effective and why. You should consider the details each writer gives about the town, the words and phrases they use and how their language conveys their feelings about the town. Make sure that you refer closely to both extracts in your answer.

The following passages are concerned with issues relating to the use of nuclear power throughout the world and refer to the accidents at Chernobyl in 1986 and at Fukushima in 2011. The first two extracts are from the website of Greenpeace, an environmental organisation opposed to the use of nuclear power; the third extract consists of educational material taken from the website of the World Nuclear Association, which represents people throughout the world involved in the nuclear profession. The writers of both sets of material clearly hold strong views and give arguments supporting their beliefs.

Read both the Greenpeace passages carefully and then answer the questions on page 36. These questions will help you to consider how the writers set out to persuade readers to support their views.

Greenpeace 1: Push for no new nukes

Nuclear power is neither safe nor clean. There is no such thing as a 'safe' dose of radiation and just because nuclear pollution is invisible doesn't mean it's 'clean'.

If a meltdown were to occur, the accident could kill and injure tens of thousands of people, leaving large regions uninhabitable. And, more than 50 years after splitting the first atom, science has yet to devise a method for adequately handling long-lived radioactive wastes.

For years nuclear plants have been leaking radioactive waste from underground pipes and radioactive waste pools into the ground water at sites across the UK.

In order to save the future of our planet, we must continue to fight the expansion of nuclear power and instead push for clean, renewable sources of energy.

Greenpeace 2: Chernobyl – distorted reality and unanswered questions

Blogpost by Iris Cheng – 21 April 2011

We have just returned after completing an important mission in Ukraine – taking around 70 journalists from 18 countries with us to Chernobyl, nearly 25 years after the nuclear catastrophe. It was one of the largest media trips Greenpeace has organised. These seasoned journalists asked critical and insightful questions, none of them were easily moved.

But many of them were deeply disturbed by what they saw and heard – often by the mundane details that were mentioned matter-of-factly by the interviewees.

Like how every year the Ukraine government needs to spend between six and eight per cent of the fiscal budget to cope with the consequences of Chernobyl.

Like how tens of thousands of Ukrainian children need to be sent away every year to uncontaminated areas for at least a month, in order to allow the body to get rid of some of the caesium-137 accumulated through eating everyday food like milk, mushrooms, berry jam and meat.

Like how food sold in every market needs to be tested for radionuclide like caesium and strontium.

Like how children of Rokytne get tonsillitis several times a year because their immune systems are compromised by radionuclide. According to the deputy head doctor from the District Hospital, two thirds of the population of 53 000 he cares for are affected by caesium-137 contamination in food. Rokytne is 300 km away from Chernobyl, on the other side of the country.

Like how the local health and sanitary stations in some areas need to make maps to tell local communities where the radiation hotspots are and [it's] thus unsafe to go.

Like how in school, children are taught the practical steps of radiation safety, and do emergency drills with gas masks.

Like how young expectant mothers get advice about what food they need to avoid, in order to minimise radionuclide uptake, which causes deformity in the developing foetus. They need frequent checks and if the foetus develops serious deformity then it may have to be aborted.

Like how it is considered impolite to ask workers building the new sarcophagus about their personal radiation dose. If it reaches the limit then they cannot work, which means they lose their job.

Like how radioactive waste containment and management had become an important sector of the economy, because of the Chernobyl disaster. The original sarcophagus, hastily built in the months after the accident, is meant to only last 25–30 years and is now at risk of collapse. Underneath, the destroyed reactor is still on site and cannot be dismantled because of its extreme radioactivity.

The consequences of the Chernobyl nuclear disaster lie in these mundane everyday facts. Life for these communities is brutally distorted, for centuries to come.

||||➡

However, when I returned from Ukraine, I was hit by another distorted reality. Nuclear proponents now claim that – despite the fact that the situation in the Fukushima nuclear plant is still not under control, despite the massive amount of radioactive water dumped into the sea with unknown consequences – Fukushima proves that nuclear energy is safe, because so far no one has been killed by the radiation.

I want them to say that to the [Ukrainian] doctors and parents who are told that the state can now only afford to send children away for breaks in clean areas for 18 days per year. Nuclear supporters probably don't know that it takes 50 days for the body of a child (100 days for adult) to get rid of half of its radioactive caesium-137.

I want them to say that to the public health officials who are struggling to find funding to continue monitoring food contamination.

I want them to say that to the young woman who told us her favourite fruit is the blueberries from the forests. She knows they are contaminated by caesium but she cannot help eating them sometimes.

I want them to take human life more seriously. There are 442 nuclear power plants in the world today and the majority are ageing. There will be leaks, power outages, human errors, design flaws. The nuclear industry has no solutions to the radioactive waste problem. How many more life-crippling nuclear disasters will it take before the world gets rid of this outdated, dangerous and unnecessary technology?

Exercise 2: Greenpeace 1 and 2

1 From the first extract – 'Push for no new nukes' – give three criticisms made of nuclear power.

2 From the first extract, explain, in your own words, what Greenpeace's attitude is to nuclear power.

3 By referring closely to the content of the blogpost about the visit to Chernobyl and the language used, explain fully how this passage sets out to persuade readers both to sympathise with the people in the area and to support the arguments against nuclear power.

4 Why do you think Iris Cheng makes specific reference to the fact that the visit was made by 'seasoned journalists' who were not 'easily moved'?

5 Explain the meaning of 'radionuclide' and 'sarcophagus' as used in the blog. You can use a dictionary or other reference book.

6 From the whole passage about Chernobyl, write a summary of the effects of the disaster on people still living in the area and what the writer considers to be the most important points for the rest of the world to learn. You should write about 150 words and use your own words as far as possible.

7 Consider the use both Greenpeace passages make of facts, opinions and opinions presented as facts. Give examples of all of these and explain how they contribute (or not) to persuading readers to support the Greenpeace campaign.

Now read this passage and then answer the questions that follow on page 39.

World Nuclear Association: Overview of nuclear energy

The main use of nuclear energy is to generate electricity. This is simply a clean and efficient way of boiling water to make steam which drives turbine generators. Except for the reactor itself, a nuclear power station works like most coal- or gas-fired power stations. The fuel for it is basically uranium.

Why use nuclear energy to make the steam?

Because it is clean, safe, and usually cost-competitive. And because very little fuel is needed, countries can store a few years' supply easily and cheaply. Energy security is increasingly a factor.

Originally it was because it was seen as more convenient and probably cheaper than fossil-fuel alternatives such as coal, gas and oil. That was when the technology was first developed for harnessing the power of the atom in a safe and controlled manner, in the 1950s. Since then the question of sustainability has emerged, giving rise to a more sophisticated rationale.

Nuclear energy has distinct environmental advantages over fossil fuels, in that virtually all its wastes are contained and managed – nuclear power stations do not cause any pollution. The fuel for nuclear power is virtually unlimited, considering both geological and technological aspects. That is to say, there is plenty of uranium in the Earth's crust and furthermore, well-proven (but not yet fully economic) technology means that we can extract about 60 times as much energy from it as we do today. The safety record of nuclear energy is better than for any major industrial technology.

Nuclear energy supplies some 14% of the world's electricity, more than the world used from all sources in 1960. Today 30 countries use nuclear energy to generate up to three quarters of their electricity, and a substantial number of these depend on it for one quarter to one half of their supply. Some 14 000 reactor years of operational experience have been accumulated since the 1950s by the world's 440 nuclear power reactors (and nuclear reactors powering naval vessels have clocked up a similar amount).

Safety

From the outset, safety of nuclear reactors has been a very high priority in their design and engineering. About one third of the cost of a typical reactor is due to safety systems and structures. The Chernobyl accident in 1986 was a reminder of the importance of this, whereas the Three Mile Island accident in 1979 showed that conventional safety systems work. The Fukushima accident in 2011 also showed that even a triple accident due to an unprecedented natural disaster was largely contained on site.

At Chernobyl in Ukraine 30 people were killed (mostly by high levels of radiation) and many more injured or adversely affected. This reactor lacked the basic engineering provisions necessary for licensing in most parts of the world (other reactors of that kind still operating have been significantly modified). At Three Mile Island in the USA with a similarly serious malfunction, the effects were contained and no one suffered any harm or injury.

Wastes

Nuclear power produces wastes which are contained and managed, with the cost of this being met by the electricity customer at the time. It does not produce any significant wastes which are dispersed to the environment. It therefore avoids contributing to increased carbon-dioxide levels in the atmosphere, or other environmental effects.

The main wastes produced by 'burning' uranium in a nuclear reactor are very hot and radioactive, placing them among the most unpleasant wastes from modern industry. However, these 'high-level' nuclear wastes are modest in quantity. Handling and storing them safely is quite straightforward, they simply need to be shielded from human exposure, and cooled. Shielding can be by water, concrete, steel or other dense material, cooling is by air or water. For instance, when used fuel is removed from a typical reactor, it is done under water and the used fuel is transferred to a large storage pool where it may remain for up to 50 years.

Other radioactive wastes also arise from the nuclear fuel cycle; these have greater volume but are more easily handled and disposed of. One characteristic of all radioactive wastes which distinguishes them from the very much larger amount of other industrial wastes is that their radioactivity progressively decays and diminishes. For instance, after 40 years, the used fuel removed from a reactor has only one thousandth of its initial radioactivity remaining, making it very much easier to handle and dispose of.

Civil nuclear wastes have never caused any harm, nor posed an environmental hazard, in over 50 years of the nuclear power industry.

Other uses

Although this website focuses on the use of nuclear energy to produce electricity, it is important to note that nuclear energy is also used to produce the radioisotopes used in many parts of our modern world, with health services, industry and even domestic safety very dependent on them. Many homes have smoke detectors which depend on a tiny amount of americium, derived from plutonium made in a nuclear reactor. In the developed countries, about one half of all people will depend on nuclear medicine at some stage of their lives.

Exercise 3: World Nuclear Association

1 Explain fully, using your own words, why nuclear energy is used to make steam.
2 By referring to paragraph 4 (beginning 'Nuclear energy has distinct ...'), explain, using your own words, the advantages of nuclear energy over other fuels.
3 How does the passage set out to persuade you that using nuclear energy is safe?
4 Write a summary of about 80–100 words of how radioactive waste is disposed of and why the procedures for doing so are not harmful. You should use your own words as far as possible.

Exercise 4: Comparing the Greenpeace and World Nuclear Association passages

Write a detailed comparison of the passages from Greenpeace and the World Nuclear Association. In your answer you should:
- explain clearly the intentions of each passage
- explain how the content of each passage and the tone created by the words and phrases used by each writer will influence readers (remember to quote examples)
- explain which organisation's material you find more effective and why.

Reading for pleasure

So far you have looked only at how the written word is used to persuade people but the effect of the spoken word can be equally great. Here is an extract from a famous speech made by the American Civil Rights activist Martin Luther King to his supporters in 1963. (You may wish to find a recording of the actual speech by searching on the internet.)

'I have a dream'

Nineteen sixty-three is not an end but a beginning …

There are those who are asking the devotees of civil rights, 'When will you be satisfied?' We can never be satisfied as long as the negro is the victim of the unspeakable horrors of police brutality.

We can never be satisfied as long as our bodies, heavy with the fatigue of travel, cannot gain lodging in the motels of the highways and the hotels of the cities.

We cannot be satisfied as long as the negro's basic mobility is from a smaller ghetto to a larger one.

We can never be satisfied as long as our children are stripped of their selfhood and robbed of their dignity by signs stating 'For whites only'.

We cannot be satisfied as long as a negro in Mississippi cannot vote and a negro in New York believes he has nothing for which to vote.

No, no we are not satisfied, and we will not be satisfied until justice rolls down like waters and righteousness like a mighty stream.

I am not unmindful that some of you have come here out of great trials and tribulations. Some of you have come fresh from narrow jail cells. Some of you have come from areas where your quest for freedom left you battered by the storms of persecution and staggered by the winds of police brutality.

You have been the veterans of creative suffering. Continue to work with the faith that unearned suffering is redemptive.

Go back to Mississippi, go back to Alabama, go back to South Carolina, go back to Georgia, go back to Louisiana, go back to the slums and ghettos of our northern cities, knowing that somehow this situation can and will be changed.

Let us not wallow in the valley of despair. I say to you today, my friends, so even though we face the difficulties of today and tomorrow, I still have a dream. It is a dream deeply rooted in the American dream.

I have a dream that one day this nation will rise up and live out the true meaning of its creed: 'We hold these truths to be self-evident that all men are created equal.'

I have a dream that one day, on the red hills of Georgia, the sons of former slaves and the sons of former slave owners will be able to sit down together at the table of brotherhood.

I have a dream that one day even the state of Mississippi, a state sweltering with the heat of injustice, sweltering with the heat of oppression, will be transformed into an oasis of freedom and justice.

I have a dream that my four little children will one day live in a nation where they will not be judged by the colour of their skin but by the content of their character.

I have a dream today.

I have a dream that one day down in Alabama, with its vicious racists, with its governor having his lips dripping with the words of interposition and nullification, one day right down in Alabama, little black boys and black girls will be able to join hands with little white boys and white girls as sisters and brothers.

I have a dream today.

I have a dream that one day every valley shall be exalted, every hill and mountain shall be made low, the rough places will be made plain and the crooked places will be made straight, and the glory of the Lord shall be revealed and all flesh shall see it together.

This is our hope. This is the faith that I go back to the south with. With this faith we will be able to hew out of the mountain of despair a stone of hope. With this faith we will be able to transform the jangling discords of our nation into a beautiful symphony of brotherhood. With this faith we will be able to work together, to pray together, to struggle together, to go to jail together, to stand up for freedom together, knowing that we will be free one day.

This will be the day, this will be the day when all of God's children will be able to sing with new meaning 'My country 'tis of thee, sweet land of liberty, of thee I sing. Land where my fathers died, land of the pilgrim's pride, from every mountainside, let freedom ring!'

And if America is to be a great nation, this must become true. So let freedom ring from the prodigious hilltops of New Hampshire. Let freedom ring from the mighty mountains of New York.

||||➡

Let freedom ring from the heightening Alleghenies of Pennsylvania.

Let freedom ring from the snow-capped Rockies of Colorado.

Let freedom ring from the curvaceous slopes of California.

But not only that, let freedom ring from Stone Mountain of Georgia.

Let freedom ring from Lookout Mountain of Tennessee.

Let freedom ring from every hill and molehill of Mississippi, from every mountainside.

Let freedom ring.

And when this happens, and when we allow freedom ring, when we let it ring from every village and every hamlet, from every state and every city, we will be able to speed up that day when *all* of God's children, black men and white men, Jews and Gentiles, Protestants and Catholics, will be able to join hands and sing in the words of the old negro spiritual: 'Free at last, free at last. Thank God Almighty, we are free at last.'

Martin Luther King

Writing

Activity

There is a proposal to build a brand-new sports and leisure centre in the area where you live. This is a much-needed facility and will benefit all members of your community. It will also provide jobs for local people. However, building the leisure centre will mean closing a day centre for old people and relocating it in new premises a few kilometres away. The new leisure centre is also likely to increase noise and traffic problems in what is an already busy area. There is considerable disagreement among local people as to whether the leisure centre should be built or not.

Decide whether you are in favour of the leisure centre being built or against it and in favour of retaining the old people's day centre. Write the words of a speech to your class group in which you would try strongly to persuade them to support your point of view. Remember that you should try to persuade them both through the content of your speech and the language you use.

Group activity

Your school is planning to hold a fund-raising day and your headteacher/principal is running a competition to decide which organisations the money raised should be donated to. A prize will be given to the group of students who produce the best campaign on behalf of their chosen organisation. Your group strongly supports raising money for one of the organisations that are trying to save tigers from extinction.

Working in your group, produce your entry for the school competition. For example, you should create leaflets intended to inform and explain and a written proposal saying why you believe saving tigers is so important. Use details from the passages that follow on pages 43–44 and any other material that you are able to research yourselves to help you persuade people to support your chosen organisation.

Tigers: overview

Possibly as few as 3200 left in the wild

Facts and figures

- Tigers are found in Bangladesh, Bhutan, Cambodia, China, India, Indonesia (Sumatra), Laos, Malaysia, Myanmar, Nepal, Russia (Far East), Thailand and Vietnam.
- The six living subspecies of tigers are: Amur, Bengal, Indochinese, Malayan, South China and Sumatran.
- The Bali, Caspian and Javan tiger subspecies have all become extinct.
- Wild-tiger numbers have fallen by about 95% over the past 100 years.
- Tigers survive in an area 40% smaller than they occupied a decade ago.

Tigers are the largest of all the Asian big cats, at the top the food chain, and are one of the most culturally important and beautiful animals on this planet. However, they are also among the most vulnerable and threatened species on Earth.

For over a million years, the 'King of the Jungle' lorded over a territory stretching from eastern Turkey to the Russian Far East, with its home extending northward to Siberia and southward into Bali. But by the end of the last century, the Bali, Javan and Caspian tigers were extinct. Tragically, the remaining six subspecies risk the same fate as the Javan and Caspian because of illegal wildlife trade, poaching, and conflict with people.

If we do not respond to the plight of wild tigers and the needs of the communities that share their home with tigers – most of which is outside protected wildlife areas – we will witness the loss of one of the world's most irreplaceable natural wonders of our lifetime.

Subspecies

Three tiger subspecies – the Bali, Javan, and Caspian – have become extinct in the past 70 years. The six remaining subspecies – Amur, Bengal, Indochinese, Malayan, South China, and Sumatran – live only in Asia, and all are threatened by poaching and habitat loss.

Amur (Siberian) Tiger
Scientific name: *Panthera tigris altaica*
IUCN Listing: Endangered
Habitat: Coniferous, scrub oak and birch woodlands
Location: Primarily eastern Russia, with a few found in north-eastern China

World Wildlife Fund (WWF)

Siberian tigers

It is estimated that the wild population of Siberian tigers stands at around 350–450 tigers.

Almost all wild Siberian tigers live in the south-east corner of Russia in the Sikhote-Alin mountain range east of the Amur River. Their former range included north-eastern China and the Korean Peninsula, and as far west as Mongolia. They are the largest of the tiger species and can grow up to 13 feet (4 m) in length and weigh up to 700 lb (300 kg).

The Siberian – or Amur – tiger is considered a critically **endangered species** with the primary threats to its survival in the wild being poaching and habitat loss from intensive logging and development.

Tigers are most commonly poached for their fur and for their body parts used in Traditional Chinese Medicine. It is estimated that in 1991 alone, one third of the Siberian tiger population was killed to meet the demand for their bones and other parts used in this practice. This even though the practice is now unlawful in China.

In 1993 the State Council of the People's Republic of China issued a notice declaring the use of tiger bone for medicinal purposes to be illegal. The Chinese government encouraged the Ministry of Public Health and the pharmaceutical companies to seek substitute medicines for tiger parts.

However, because it is such a lucrative trade – a single tiger can bring up to $50 000 on the international market – the practice is still flourishing.

The other vital concern for the survival of the Siberian tiger in the wild is habitat loss.

Research has demonstrated the Siberian tigers require vast forest landscapes to survive. However, logging, both legal and illegal, is threatening the tigers' home by fragmenting their habitat thereby isolating them from each other. In addition, the continuous creation of new logging roads provides poachers with access to formerly remote areas.

So, in essence, for the Siberian tiger to survive in the wild, and no longer be considered an endangered species, two things must happen. First, habitat encroachment must stop and secondly, the thousands-of-years-old tradition of using tiger parts for medicinal purposes must also end.

Tigers in Crisis

Speaking and listening

> Group activity
>
> As part of your attempt to win the prize for the school fund-raising day in the group activity on pages 42–43, your group has been asked to present your ideas to the judges and explain why you believe that your campaign is important. Role play the interview with some members of the group playing the judges and others presenting the arguments in favour of your campaign.

Key skills

Verbs

Gerunds

Participles and infinitives, which we learnt about in Chapters 1 and 2, are known as non-finite parts of the verb. However, there is one further non-finite part of the verb to consider: the **gerund** or **verbal noun**. As the alternative name suggests, the gerund functions grammatically as a noun.

The gerund takes the same form as the present participle, so the gerund of the verb *to sing* is *singing*. It can be used in a sentence as either the subject or the object of another verb. For example:

Singing is an enjoyable activity.

I enjoy *singing*.

As it functions as a noun, a gerund can be described by an adjective. For example:

Choral singing is a very enjoyable activity.

Although the gerund functions as a noun, it still retains its character as a verb. Here is an example:

Eating vegetables is good for you.

In this sentence, the gerund *eating* is the subject of the verb *is* (and is, therefore, doing the work of a noun) but also has its own object, *vegetables*, and so retains its verbal function. Similarly, in the following example the gerund *scraping* has its own adverb, *noisily*, describing its action as a verb:

Noisily scraping your plate can spoil other people's enjoyment of the meal.

Note that as the gerund is a noun, it must be accompanied by a possessive adjective and not by a personal pronoun. This is a common confusion and error of expression. For example, there is a significant difference between these sentences:

> I don't like *his* singing. ✓

> I don't like *him* singing. ✗

The first sentence means that it is the person's singing that I dislike; it does not tell us that I dislike the person himself. The second sentence is grammatically incorrect, but if it meant anything, it would mean that I don't like the person who happens to be singing.

Vocabulary

Exercise: Word associations

When looking at how writers set out to persuade readers to share their point of view, we considered how choosing particular words can influence readers' responses. Below are ten words which all relate to impressions received by your nose. Which suggest to you the worst and which the most pleasant smells? Order the words on a scale of 1 to 10 from worst to most pleasant.

> aroma bouquet fragrance odour perfume
> smell stench stink tang whiff

Now compare your results with those of other members of your class – you may be surprised at the outcome. In particular, think about the associations attached to the different words.

Creating descriptions

Reading

We have already looked at ways of writing descriptively in *Student's Books 1* and *2*. Descriptive writing is an important requirement of the Checkpoint tests that you will be taking, so in this chapter we will consider further examples, both in poetry and in prose.

One of the key features of a good piece of writing, no matter what its purpose, is that it should be convincing to its readers. A work of fiction is unlikely to be successful if readers are unable to believe in either the characters about whom the story is being told, or the setting in which the story takes place. Similarly, informative or personal pieces of writing are unlikely to hold readers' interest unless they convey clear and credible information and details. It is particularly important that a poet who is attempting to recreate an experience that can be shared with readers describes that experience in a way that is both honest and convincing.

All writing communicates with readers through the medium of words. In the passages and exercises in this chapter, we will be exploring how the words chosen by the writers convey their thoughts and feelings.

Two poems describing places

The two poems that follow both describe places that are well known to the poets. In 'The Lake Isle of Innisfree', William Butler Yeats describes a quiet, almost magical, place in the Irish countryside that he visits when he wishes for peace and solitude and the opportunity to escape from the pressures of city life. In fact, his memories of this place are so strong that he can escape there in his mind when he feels things are getting too much for him. In contrast, in the second poem (on pages 49–50) John Betjeman describes a beach in the English county of Cornwall which, although well known to him, here takes on a sinister and threatening atmosphere.

Read Yeats's poem carefully and then answer the questions that follow. Some words printed in italics have been explained for you to the right of the poem.

'The Lake Isle of Innisfree'

I will arise and go now, and go to Innisfree,
And a small cabin build there, of clay and *wattles* made;
Nine bean rows will I have there, a hive for the honey bee,
   And live alone in the bee-loud glade.

rods or stakes interwoven with twigs or tree branches for making fences, walls, etc.

And I shall have some peace there, for peace comes dropping slow,
Dropping from the veils of the morning to where the cricket sings;
There midnight's all a glimmer, and noon a purple glow,
   And evening full of the *linnet's* wings.

small bird of finch family

I will arise and go now, for always night and day
I hear lake water lapping with low sounds by the shore;
While I stand on the roadway, or on the pavements grey,
   I hear it in the deep heart's core.

W.B. Yeats

Exercise 1: 'The Lake Isle of Innisfree'

1 Explain, using your own words, what the poet tells us that he intends to do in the first four lines of the poem.
2 Explore fully and comment on the imagery in the phrase 'the veils of the morning'.
3 Suggest reasons why midnight might be 'all a glimmer' and noon 'a purple glow'.
4 Why do you think that the poet chose to invert the usual word order in the phrase 'pavements grey'?

5 Explain as fully as you can the contrast between the last four lines and the rest of the poem. You should consider not just what the lines mean but also the language used by the poet.

6 The poet sees Innisfree as a place of peace and solitude. By referring closely to the language of the first two stanzas of the poem, explain as fully as you can how he creates the atmosphere of the island and its sights and sounds. You should consider, in particular, the poem's rhythm, its use of rhyme and onomatopoeia.

Now read John Betjeman's poem carefully and answer the questions that follow. Some words printed in italics have been explained for you to the right of the poem.

'Greenaway'

I know so well this *turfy* mile,	grassy
These clumps of *sea-pink* withered brown,	flowering plant found near sea
The breezy cliff, the awkward stile,	
The sandy path that takes me down.	
To crackling layers of broken slate	
Where black and flat sea-woodlice crawl	
And isolated rock pools wait	
Wash from the highest tides of all.	
I know the roughly blasted track	
That skirts a small and smelly bay	
And over squelching *bladderwrack*	type of seaweed
Leads to the beach at Greenaway.	

Down on the shingle safe at last
I hear the slowly dragging roar
As mighty rollers mount to cast
Small coal and seaweed on the shore,

And spurting far as it can reach
The shooting surf comes hissing round
To heave a line along the beach
Of *cowries* waiting to be found.   type of shell

Tide after tide by night and day
The breakers battle with the land
And rounded smooth along the bay
The faithful rocks protecting stand.

But in a dream the other night
I saw this coastline from the sea
And felt the breakers plunging white
Their weight of waters over me.

There were the stile, the turf, the shore,
The safety line of shingle beach
With every stroke I struck the more
The backwash sucked me out of reach.

Back into what a water-world
Of waving weed and waiting claws?
Of writhing tentacles uncurled
To drag me to what dreadful jaws?

John Betjeman

Exercise 2: 'Greenaway'

1 By referring closely to the first three stanzas of 'Greenaway', describe as fully as you can, using your own words, the path to the shingle beach.
2 Why do you think that the poet says that he is 'safe at last' when he reaches the shingle?
3 Compare the description of the sea in stanzas 4–6 with the description of the path in stanzas 1–3.
4 Explore how the poet's choice of words and images in stanzas 4–6 helps to suggest the sounds and appearance of the sea.
5 Explain as fully as you can, using your own words, the experience described by the poet in the last three stanzas of the poem. In particular, what effects are achieved by the questions in the last stanza?
6 Considering the poem as a whole, what message do you think the poet is conveying about the way we look at familiar, natural scenery?

Exercise 3: Comparing the poems

Write a detailed comparison of the two poems. You should consider:

- the ways in which they present the places they describe
- the atmosphere the poets create
- the different points of view of the poets
- the words and language that they use.

Two descriptions of dark interiors

Both of the following passages describe dark and rather unpleasant scenes inside buildings. The first is taken from a short story called 'Games at Twilight' by Anita Desai and describes the inside of a shed in a garden in India. In the story, a group of children are playing hide and seek. In this extract, the timid Ravi is hiding from the hunter, Raghu.

Read the passage carefully and then answer the questions that follow on page 53.

The shed

But next to the garage was another shed with a big green door. Also locked. No one even knew who had the key to the lock. That shed wasn't opened more than once a year when Ma turned out all the old broken bits of furniture and rolls of matting and leaking buckets, and the white ant hills were broken and swept away and Flit [an insecticide] sprayed into the spider webs and rat holes so that the whole operation was like the looting of a poor, ruined and conquered city. The green leaves of the door sagged. They were nearly off their rusty hinges. The hinges were large and made a small gap between the door and the walls – only just large enough for rats, dogs and, possibly, Ravi to slip through.

Ravi had never cared to enter such a dark and depressing mortuary of defunct household goods seething with such unspeakable and alarming animal life but, as Raghu's whistling grew angrier and sharper and his crashing and storming in the hedge wilder, Ravi suddenly slipped off the flower pot and through the crack and was gone. He chuckled aloud with astonishment at his own temerity so that Raghu came out of the hedge, stood silent with his hands on his hips, listening, and finally shouted 'I heard you! I'm coming! Got you –' and came charging round the garage only to find the upturned flower pot, the yellow dust, the crawling of white ants in a mud-hill against the closed shed door – nothing. Snarling, he bent to pick up a stick and went off, whacking it against the garage and shed walls as if to beat out his prey.

** ||||➡

Ravi shook, then shivered with delight, with self-congratulation. Also with fear. It was dark, spooky in the shed. It had a muffled smell, as of graves. Ravi had once got locked into the linen cupboard and sat there weeping for half an hour before he was rescued. But at least that had been a familiar place, and even smelt pleasantly of starch, laundry and, reassuringly, of his mother. But the shed smelt of rats, ant hills, dust and spider webs. Also of less definable, less recognisable horrors. And it was dark. Except for the white-hot cracks, along the door, there was no light. The roof was very low. Although Ravi was small, he felt as if he could reach up and touch it with his fingertips. But he didn't stretch. He hunched himself into a ball so as not to bump into anything, touch or feel anything. What might there not be to touch him and feel him as he stood there, trying to see in the dark? Something cold, or slimy – like a snake. Snakes! He leapt up as Raghu whacked the wall with his stick – then, quickly realising what it was, felt almost relieved to hear Raghu, hear his stick. It made him feel protected.

But Raghu soon moved away. There wasn't a sound once his footsteps had gone around the garage and disappeared. Ravi stood frozen inside the shed. Then he shivered all over. Something had tickled the back of his neck. It took him a while to pick up the courage to lift his hand and explore. It was an insect – perhaps a spider – exploring him. He squashed it and wondered how many more creatures were watching him, waiting to reach out and touch him, the stranger.

There was nothing now. After standing in that position – his hand still on his neck, feeling the wet splodge of the squashed spider gradually dry – for minutes, hours, his legs began to tremble with the effort, the inaction. By now he could see enough in the dark to make out the large solid shapes of old wardrobes, broken buckets and bedsteads piled on top of each other around him. He recognised an old bathtub – patches of enamel glimmered at him and at last he lowered himself onto its edge.

Anita Desai

Exercise 4: The shed

1 Explain how Ravi managed to enter the shed.

2 Give the meaning of the following phrases as used in the second paragraph: 'a dark and depressing mortuary of defunct household goods'; 'astonishment at his own temerity'.

3 By referring closely to the third paragraph, explain Ravi's state of mind and what he found disturbing about the inside of the shed.

4 Find three examples from the passage that tell you that Ravi is a timid child. Give reasons for your choices.

5 Do you think that Ravi's feelings change in the final paragraph? Give reasons for your answer and refer closely to the passage.

6 The shed contains nothing more than old household goods and yet the writer's account of Ravi's experience turns it into somewhere scary and threatening. Explain as fully as you can how the writer achieves this effect. You should consider the descriptions of the inside of the shed, the things that are in it and, in particular, Ravi's feelings and how he reacts to his situation.

7 Write your own continuation and conclusion of the story. Try to continue in the same style as the original and use clues from the passage to help you imagine what might happen next.

The next passage is taken from an autobiographical work, *Down and Out in Paris and London*, in which George Orwell tells of his first day working in the kitchens of a top Paris hotel in the 1930s. Read this extract carefully and then answer the question that follows on page 55.

The kitchens of the Hotel X

He led me down a winding staircase into a narrow passage, deep underground, and so low that I had to stoop in places. It was stiflingly hot and very dark, with only dim, yellow bulbs several yards apart. There seemed to be miles of dark labyrinthine passages – actually, I suppose, a few hundred yards in all – that reminded one queerly of the lower decks of a liner; there were the same heat and cramped space and warm reek of food, and a humming, whirring noise (it came from the kitchen furnaces) just like the whir of engines. We passed doorways which let out sometimes a shouting of oaths, sometimes the red glare of a fire, once a shuddering draught from an ice chamber. As we went along, something struck me violently in the back. It was a hundred-pound [40 kg] block of ice, carried by a blue-aproned porter. After him came a boy with a great slab of veal on his shoulder, his cheek pressed into the damp, spongy flesh. They shoved me aside with a cry of '*Sauve-toi, idiot!*' ['Watch out, you idiot!'] and rushed on ...

One of the passages branched off into a laundry, where an old, skull-faced woman gave me a blue apron and a pile of dishcloths. Then the *chef du personnel* took me to a tiny underground den – a cellar below a cellar, as it were – where there were a sink and some

gas-ovens. It was too low for me to stand quite upright, and the temperature was perhaps 110 degrees Fahrenheit [over 40 °C]. The *chef du personnel* explained that my job was to fetch meals for the higher hotel employees, who fed in a small dining-room above, clean their room and wash their crockery. When he had gone, a waiter, another Italian, thrust a fierce, fuzzy head into the doorway and looked down at me.

'English, eh?' he said. 'Well, I'm in charge here. If you work well' – he made the motion of up-ending a bottle and sucked noisily. 'If you don't'– he gave the doorpost several vigorous kicks. 'To me, twisting your neck would be no more than spitting on the floor. And if there's any trouble, they'll believe me, not you. So be careful.'

After this I set to work rather hurriedly. Except for about an hour, I was at work from seven in the morning till a quarter past nine at night; first at washing crockery, then at scrubbing the tables and floors of the employees' dining-room, then at polishing glasses and knives, then at fetching meals, then at washing crockery again, then at fetching more meals and washing more crockery. It was easy work, and I got on well with it except when I went to the kitchen to fetch meals. The kitchen was like nothing I had ever seen or imagined – a stifling, low-ceilinged inferno of a cellar, red-lit from the fires, and deafening with oaths and the clanging of pots and pans. It was so hot that all the metal-work except the stoves had to be covered with cloth. In the middle were furnaces, where twelve cooks skipped to and fro, their faces dripping sweat in spite of their white caps. Round that were counters where a mob of waiters and *plongeurs* [dishwashers] clamoured with trays. Scullions, naked to the waist, were stoking the fires and scouring huge copper saucepans with sand. Everyone seemed to be in a hurry and a rage. The head cook, a fine, scarlet man with big moustachios, stood in the middle booming continuously, '*Ça marche deux oeufs brouillés! Ça marche un Chateaubriand aux pommes sautées!*' ['Let's go, two scrambled eggs! Let's go, a Chateaubriand steak with fried potatoes!'] except when he broke off to curse at a *plongeur*. There were three counters, and the first time I went to the kitchen I took my tray unknowingly to the wrong one. The head cook walked up to me, twisted his moustaches, and looked me up and down. Then he beckoned to the breakfast cook and pointed at me.

'Do you see THAT? That is the type of *plongeur* they send us nowadays. Where do you come from, idiot? From Charenton, I suppose?' [There is a large lunatic asylum at Charenton.]

George Orwell

Exercise 5: The kitchens of the Hotel X

By referring closely to the passage, explore how George Orwell brings to life the kitchens of the Hotel X. In your answer you should write about the author's use of descriptive language, especially in the first and fourth paragraphs. You should also consider how his descriptions of the other people working in the kitchen and his account of what he himself did and how he was treated add to the picture he creates.

Description of a living creature

In the following poem, the poet describes an event which happened to him while living on the Mediterranean island of Sicily. Through carefully chosen words and images he vividly recreates his encounter with a snake, as well as using the experience to analyse his own response. Read the poem carefully and then answer the questions that follow.

'Snake'

A snake came to my water-trough
On a hot, hot day, and I in pyjamas for the heat,
To drink there.

In the deep, strange-scented shade of the great dark carob-tree
I came down the steps with my pitcher
And must wait, must stand and wait, for there he was at the trough before me.

He reached down from a fissure in the earth-wall in the gloom
And trailed his yellow-brown slackness soft-bellied down, over the edge of the stone trough
And rested his throat upon the stone bottom,
And where the water had dripped from the tap, in a small clearness,
He sipped with his straight mouth,
Softly drank through his straight gums, into his slack long body,
Silently.

Someone was before me at my water-trough,
And I, like a second comer, waiting.

He lifted his head from his drinking, as cattle do,
And looked at me vaguely, as drinking cattle do,
And flickered his two-forked tongue from his lips,
 and mused a moment,
And stooped and drank a little more,
Being earth-brown, earth-golden from the burning
 bowels of the earth
On the day of Sicilian July, with Etna smoking.
The voice of my education said to me
He must be killed,
For in Sicily the black, black snakes are innocent,
 the gold are venomous.

And voices in me said, If you were a man
You would take a stick and break him now, and
 finish him off.

But must I confess how I liked him,
How glad I was he had come like a guest in quiet,
 to drink at my water-trough
And depart peaceful, pacified, and thankless,
Into the burning bowels of this earth.

Was it cowardice, that I dared not kill him? Was it
 perversity, that I longed to talk to him?
Was it humility, to feel so honoured?
I felt so honoured.

And yet those voices:
If you were not afraid, you would kill him!

And truly I was afraid, I was most afraid, But even so, honoured still more
That he should seek my hospitality
From out the dark door of the secret earth.

He drank enough
And lifted his head, dreamily, as one who has drunken,
And flickered his tongue like a forked night on the air, so black,
Seeming to lick his lips,
And looked around like a god, unseeing, into the air,
And slowly turned his head,
And slowly, very slowly, as if thrice adream,
Proceeded to draw his slow length curving round
And climb again the broken bank of my wall-face.

And as he put his head into that dreadful hole,
And as he slowly drew up, snake-easing his shoulders, and entered farther,
A sort of horror, a sort of protest against his withdrawing into that horrid black hole,
Deliberately going into the blackness, and slowly drawing himself after,
Overcame me now his back was turned.

I looked round, I put down my pitcher,
I picked up a clumsy log
And threw it at the water-trough with a clatter.

I think it did not hit him,
But suddenly that part of him that was left behind convulsed in undignified haste.
Writhed like lightning, and was gone
Into the black hole, the earth-lipped fissure in the wall-front,
At which, in the intense still noon, I stared with fascination.

And immediately I regretted it.
I thought how paltry, how vulgar, what a mean act!
I despised myself and the voices of my accursed human education.

And I thought of the albatross
And I wished he would come back, my snake.

For he seemed to me again like a king,
Like a king in exile, uncrowned in the underworld,
Now due to be crowned again.

And so, I missed my chance with one of the lords
Of life.
And I have something to expiate:
A pettiness.

D.H. Lawrence

> The line 'And I thought of the albatross', near the end of the
> poem, is a reference to the poem *The Rime of the Ancient
> Mariner*, by Samuel Taylor Coleridge, which describes the
> horrifying events that befall a sailor who for no reason kills an
> albatross – a bird considered by sailors to bring good luck.

Exercise 6: 'Snake'

1 What are the poet's first reactions when he sees the snake at his water-trough? You should quote from the poem in your answer.
2 Look closely at the description of the snake in stanza 3 and explain as fully as you can how the poet's language creates a picture of it in your mind.
3 In the early stages of the poem, do you think the poet is in any danger from the snake? Again, you should quote from the poem (especially from stanzas 3 and 5) in your answer.
4 What do you understand by the poet's reference to the 'voice of my education' and 'voices in me'? Explain how he reacts to these voices.
5 Why do the voices say that the poet should kill the snake and what are the poet's reasons for not wanting to?

6 Explain how the poet's language reflects the contrast between the behaviour of the snake and the attitudes suggested by the voices.

7 What reason does the poet give for throwing the log at the snake?

8 Comment on the phrase 'I picked up a clumsy log'. In what ways can a log be said to be 'clumsy'?

9 How does the rhythm of the stanza beginning 'I think it did not hit him' reflect the actions described?

10 Describe the poet's thoughts and feelings at the end of the poem, after the snake has gone. Comment particularly on what you understand by the last two lines.

11 Consider closely the language used by the poet to describe the snake and his thoughts about it in the first part of the poem, as far as the line 'And climb again the broken bank of my wall-face', and compare it with the language of the remaining stanzas. In particular, explore the effects created by the rhythm of the two sections of the poem.

Reading for pleasure

In 1842, Charles Dickens visited the USA and Canada. Here is his account of seeing the Niagara Falls for the first time and of the effect the visit had on him.

American Notes for General Circulation

We called at the town of Erie, at eight o'clock that night, and lay there an hour. Between five and six next morning, we arrived at Buffalo, where we breakfasted; and being too near the Great Falls to wait patiently anywhere else, we set off by the train, the same morning at nine o'clock, to Niagara.

It was a miserable day; chilly and raw; a damp mist falling; and the trees in that northern region quite bare and wintry. Whenever the train halted, I listened for the roar; and was constantly straining my eyes in the direction where I knew the Falls must be, from seeing the river rolling on towards them; every moment expecting to behold the spray. Within a few minutes of our stopping, not before, I saw two great white clouds rising up slowly and majestically from the depths of the earth. That was all. At length we alighted: and then for the first time, I heard the mighty rush of water, and felt the ground tremble underneath my feet.

The bank is very steep, and was slippery with rain, and half-melted ice. I hardly know how I got down, but I was soon at the bottom, and climbing, with two English officers who were crossing and had joined me, over some broken rocks, deafened by the noise, half-blinded by the spray, and wet to the skin. We were at the foot of the American Fall. I could see an immense torrent of water tearing headlong down from some great height, but had no idea of shape, or situation, or anything but vague immensity.

When we were seated in the little ferry-boat, and were crossing the swollen river immediately before both cataracts, I began to feel what it was: but I was in a manner stunned, and unable to comprehend the vastness of the scene. It was not until I came on Table Rock, and looked – Great Heaven, on what a fall of bright-green water! – that it came upon me in its full might and majesty.

Then, when I felt how near to my Creator I was standing, the first effect, and the enduring one – instant and lasting – of the tremendous spectacle, was Peace. Peace of Mind, tranquillity, calm recollections of the Dead, great thoughts of Eternal Rest and Happiness: nothing of gloom or terror. Niagara was at once stamped upon my heart, an Image of Beauty; to remain there, changeless and indelible, until its pulses cease to beat, for ever.

Oh, how the strife and trouble of daily life receded from my view, and lessened in the distance, during the ten memorable days we passed on that Enchanted Ground! What voices spoke from out the thundering water; what faces, faded from the earth, looked out upon me from its gleaming depths; what Heavenly promise glistened in those angels' tears, the drops of many hues, that showered around, and twined themselves about the gorgeous arches which the changing rainbows made!

I never stirred in all that time from the Canadian side, whither I had gone at first. I never crossed the river again; for I knew there were people on the other shore, and in such a place it is natural to shun strange company. To wander to and fro all day, and see the cataracts from all points of view; to stand upon the edge of the great Horse-Shoe Fall, marking the hurried water gathering strength as it approached the verge, yet seeming, too, to pause before it shot into the gulf below; to gaze from the river's level up at the torrent as it came streaming down; to climb the neighbouring heights and watch it through the trees, and see the wreathing water in the rapids hurrying on to take its fearful plunge; to linger in the shadow of the solemn rocks three miles [5 km] below; watching the river as, stirred by no visible cause, it heaved and eddied and awoke the echoes, being troubled yet, far down beneath the surface, by its giant leap; to have Niagara before me, lighted by the sun and by the moon, red in the day's decline, and grey as evening slowly fell upon it; to look upon it every day, and wake up in the night and hear its ceaseless voice: this was enough.

I think in every quiet season now, still do those waters roll and leap, and roar and tumble, all day long; still are the rainbows spanning them, a hundred feet [30 m] below. Still, when the sun is on them, do they shine and glow like molten gold. Still, when the day is gloomy, do they fall like snow, or seem to crumble away like the front of a great chalk cliff, or roll down the rock like dense white smoke. But always does the mighty stream appear to die as it comes down, and always from its unfathomable grave arises that tremendous ghost of spray and mist which is never laid: which has haunted this place with the same dread solemnity since Darkness brooded on the deep, and that first flood before the Deluge – Light – came rushing on Creation at the word of God.

Charles Dickens

Writing

Activity

Write your own account of how an encounter with either another living creature or with a particular place or scene influenced the way you look at the world. You may write either a prose account or a poem, but you should ensure that you describe both the creature or place concerned and the feelings that it inspired in you.

Speaking and listening

Activity

You have been asked to give a talk to your class either for or against the topic 'Poetry is an unnecessary luxury in the world of the twenty-first century'. You have 4 minutes maximum to convince them of your point of view. Give your talk.

Key skills

Errors to avoid

One thing you are likely to learn from studying poetry is the importance of choosing your words carefully and expressing your meaning precisely. This is, of course, an important point to remember in everything you write. Even the shortest and apparently most insignificant words can seriously alter the meaning of a sentence if they are carelessly used.

Exercise: If only!

Explain carefully how the different positions of the adverb 'only' can produce different meanings in these sentences:

Only Joe had a small lunch on Saturday.
Joe *only* had a small lunch on Saturday.
Joe had *only* a small lunch on Saturday.
Joe had a small lunch *only* on Saturday.
Joe had a small lunch on Saturday *only*.

How not to write poetry

So far in this chapter we have studied the work of skilled poets. The following poem is one of the *Poetic Gems* produced by William Topaz McGonagall (1825–1902) and is a notorious example of how *not* to write poetry. McGonagall was born in Dundee in Scotland and was convinced that he was a great poet. Not everyone agreed with this opinion.

This poem records McGonagall's response to a tragic train crash caused by the collapse of the bridge over the River Tay in 1879. As you read it, compare it with other poems that you have studied, and consider whether something more is required to make someone a great poet other than being able to make lines rhyme and to use high-flown 'poetic' language! Some words printed in italics have been explained for you to the right of the poem.

'The Tay Bridge Disaster'

Beautiful Railway Bridge of the Silv'ry Tay!
Alas! I am very sorry to say
That ninety lives have been taken away
On the last Sabbath day of 1879,
Which will be remember'd for a very long time.

IIII➡

'Twas about seven o'clock at night,
And the wind it blew with all its might,
And the rain came pouring down,
And the dark clouds seem'd to frown,
And the Demon of the air seem'd to say –
'I'll blow down the Bridge of Tay.'

When the train left Edinburgh
The passengers' hearts were light and felt no sorrow,
But *Boreas* blew a terrific gale,   poetic name for the north wind
Which made their hearts for to quail,
And many of the passengers with fear did say –
'I hope God will send us safe across the Bridge of Tay.'

But when the train came near to Wormit Bay,
Boreas he did loud and angry bray,
And shook the central girders of the Bridge of Tay
On the last Sabbath day of 1879,
Which will be remember'd for a very long time.

So the train sped on with all its might,
And Bonnie Dundee soon hove in sight,
And the passengers' hearts felt light,
Thinking they would enjoy themselves on the New Year,
With their friends at home they lov'd most dear,
And wish them all a happy New Year.

So the train mov'd slowly along the Bridge of Tay,
Until it was about midway,
Then the central girders with a crash gave way,
And down went the train and passengers into the Tay!
The Storm Fiend did loudly bray,
Because ninety lives had been taken away,
On the last Sabbath day of 1879,
Which will be remember'd for a very long time.

As soon as the catastrophe came to be known
The alarm from mouth to mouth was blown,
And the cry rang out all o'er the town,
Good Heavens! the Tay Bridge is blown down,
And a passenger train from Edinburgh,
Which fill'd all the people's hearts with sorrow,
And made them for to turn pale,
Because none of the passengers were sav'd to tell the tale
How the disaster happen'd on the last Sabbath day of 1879,
Which will be remember'd for a very long time.

It must have been an awful sight,
To witness in the dusky moonlight,
While the Storm Fiend did laugh, and angry did bray,
Along the Railway Bridge of the Silv'ry Tay,
Oh! ill-fated Bridge of th' Silv'ry Tay,

I must now conclude my *lay*   song
By telling the world fearlessly without the least dismay,
That your central girders would not have given way,
At least many sensible men do say,
Had they been supported on each side with buttresses,
At least many sensible men confesses,
For the stronger we our houses do build,
The less chance we have of being killed.

William Topaz McGonagall

Advertisements

Reading

Advertising is a form of using words to persuade that is all around us. There are large advertising hoardings on the side of the road as we drive past; newspapers and magazines have advertisements for a wide range of items throughout their pages; radio and television broadcasts are regularly interrupted by advertisements aimed at the audience for that particular programme. Advertising is so much a part of our lives that we tend to take it for granted and seldom give an advertisement our full attention. How then does advertising work? Are we in danger of accepting what advertisements tell us without questioning and buying what is advertised without considering either its quality or even whether it is something that we really need?

In this chapter we are going to look at how advertisements work and consider the different purposes for which advertising is used. Mainly we shall be looking at the general principles behind creating an advertisement. You may find it useful to start your own collection of advertisements to use as examples.

Why advertise?

Why is it necessary to advertise anything? What sorts of products are most frequently advertised? Where are most advertisements found? Who are the people advertisements are aimed at? What makes an advertisement successful? These are just some of the questions that we shall be considering.

When thinking about advertisements it is important to keep some key words in mind. First, there is the **target audience**. Consider the example on the right.

This is a very straightforward type of advertisement. Where would you be likely to come across something like this? Most probably you would find it either in a shop window or in the classified advertisements section of a local newspaper, where it would be placed among many similar advertisements all aimed at members of the public who might be considering buying a used car – the target audience. This type of advertisement is intended simply to draw attention to its subject (the used car for sale) and to provide some very straightforward information about it: how much the car is on sale for and

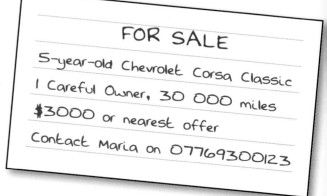

FOR SALE
5-year-old Chevrolet Corsa Classic
1 Careful Owner, 30 000 miles
$3000 or nearest offer
Contact Maria on 07769300123

the person to contact if you are interested in buying it. It makes no serious attempt to persuade you to buy the car (although the reference to one *careful* owner could be intended to do so).

Now read carefully this advertisement for a new car and then answer the questions that follow.

Can a car change you?

Mégane Renaultsport 250. 0-60 in 6.1 seconds. Cup Chassis with Limited Slip Differential. For the ultimate joie de vivre behind the wheel.

France has many Renault Mégane.
The French have high life expectancy, high fertility rates and party often.

Britain has fewer Renault Mégane.
The British eat a lot of biscuits and watch television most nights.

Is this coincidence or correlation?
Is a car the reason why France is so full of joie de vivre?

To find out if a car can really change a town, go to www.themeganeexperiment.com

DRIVE THE CHANGE

The official fuel consumption figures in mpg (l/100km) are: Urban 24.6 (11.5), Extra Urban 42.2 (6.7), Combined 33.6 (8.4). The official CO_2 emission figure is 195g/km.

Exercise 1: 'Can a car change you?'

1 This is a magazine advertisement. In what country do you think the magazine was published? Give your reasons.

2 Where are Renault cars manufactured?

3 Who do you think is the target audience for this advertisement?

4 What is meant by the phrase *joie de vivre*?

5 What effect is achieved by the question above the picture?

6 What do you understand by the phrase *national stereotypes*? Explain fully how the text of the advertisement uses national stereotypes to engage its readers. In particular, think about the tone of the language in the advertisement.

7 In what other way does the advertisement try to interest people in the Renault Mégane?

8 What information does the advertisement give you about the car itself? Do you find this particularly helpful?

9 Explain fully what you think is added to the advertisement by the photo and the graph immediately below it.

10 Explain what you think the purpose of the advertisement is. How successful do you think it is in achieving this purpose?

Now that you have answered these questions, think about how this advertisement differs from the one for the Chevrolet Corsa on page 64. The Renault Mégane advertisement is obviously intended to persuade and interest its readers; it makes use of graphic material (illustrations and headings) and its language is far more sophisticated in tone and vocabulary. In particular, consider the sentence 'Cup Chassis with Limited Slip Differential'. What does this actually mean? If, as a reader, you don't understand it, is that important? Perhaps the advertisers don't want you to understand it but would rather leave you a little confused (but also impressed) by their knowledgeable use of technical terms!

Class activity

All members of the class should bring to the lesson a newspaper or magazine advertisement and explain to their group what it is that they find particularly effective about it. The group should then discuss whether it achieves its effects more through providing information or through its entertainment value.

When each group has discussed all their different advertisements, the class should put them into categories and make a list showing how many of the examples are advertising either the same or similar products.

You might find that the most mundane items (such as toothpaste or washing powders) seem to be advertised most heavily. Why might this be the case?

Children and advertising

The passage on pages 67–69 explains ways in which advertisers target children of all ages. Read it carefully and then answer the questions that follow.

Why advertisers target children

According to research, children in the UK see around 10 000 television commercials every year. Though many advertisers claim that they advertise to reach parents rather than their kids, they're not afraid to blow multi-million-dollar marketing budgets informing children of their latest breakfast cereal, toy or console game.

So why spend so much money on advertising to children? After all – at first glance kids' spending seems to be limited to what pocket money they receive from their parents. The truth is that by investing in children when they're young, advertisers can influence parents, get access to kids' cash and create new generations of consumers who will one day introduce their own kids to the advertisers' products.

Though increasingly valuable, the 'pocket-money market' isn't the only way advertisers can make money out of children. For many years advertisers have known that even toddlers can punch way beyond their economic weight by what they call 'pester power' (also known as the 'nag factor'). With successful marketing techniques, advertisers know that kids can actively influence what their parents buy at the supermarket.

Research by psychologists shows that children can start asking parents for particular products (often by brand name) when they're as young as 24 months. Most of the time this happens while they're out shopping with parents. The research goes on to reveal that children's most-requested purchases are breakfast cereal, drinks and toys. It's not surprising that it's these items which advertisers promote with kid-friendly campaigns.

By reaching children at an early age advertisers hope to create brand loyalty that will last for the rest of the child's life. Research shows that it might be working. From the age of three kids can identify different brand logos, while a basic form of brand loyalty (e.g. choosing one kind of fast-food outlet over another) starts as early as two.

These days it's natural that parents are concerned by the sheer amount of advertising that children are exposed to on a daily basis. After all, social scientists say that modern kids can recognise over 400 company brand names by the time they reach the age of ten.

A recent survey found that 84% of parents already think that too much advertising is aimed at kids. This statistic is perhaps not surprising considering that in the modern media advertisers have more ways to reach kids than ever before. As well as the wealth of TV channels that cater solely for children (which are often watched by parents too) there is also advertising on the internet to consider as well as traditional branded books and comics.

Children today face growing up in one of the most media-saturated periods of history. From the cradle many will be watching television, while by the time they can walk they'll already be interacting with the toys seen on favourite animated TV shows – and maybe even learning the basics of the internet.

Because of the sheer proliferation of modern media, advertisers have more ways than ever to turn youngsters into young consumers through cleverly targeted adverts. The marketers' methods, whether through cartoon-like TV ads or interactive online games, seem to be working too. Psychologists have found that children who spend a lot of their time watching TV or using the internet want more of the toys that appear in ads than children who don't experience the media as much.

But how do children actually respond to the adverts that they see every day? Depending on their age and sophistication kids take on board advertisers' messages in a variety of different ways.

When they first start negotiating the world around them, children have no conception of money or buying power. Therefore they don't realise that adverts are tools designed to persuade them to want a certain product. Modern advertisers are very good at making ads that blend into the world children recognise. For instance, TV ads aimed at young kids tend to feature cartoon animals. This doesn't just appeal to toddlers because of the content (psychologists believe that children dream of animals 80% of the time), it also helps make the advert indistinguishable from the Saturday-morning cartoon programming that surrounds it. This means that younger children see TV adverts as a part of their programmes, rather than an extension.

Though they may watch up to 100 adverts for every four hours of TV programming, studies show that many children under eight have no way to critically evaluate the claims that are being made in the adverts themselves. Advertisers are excellent at producing adverts that sell their products in very emotive terms – for example surrounding breakfast cereal with an animated world that seems great fun. Children respond positively to the ads, but don't understand that the product may not be quite as exciting as the ad suggests.

As children grow older and start to be active in peer groups, advertising alters its approach. Suddenly, products (especially toys) are marketed to children as 'must-have' products. Often a happy gang of kids using the product is shown – with the subtext that children won't be accepted or liked by their peer group if they don't get the product. Psychologists have documented how this can cause tension within families and the child him/herself. 'Pester power' can make parents feel guilty if they don't buy their child the product, while kids can feel inadequate and excluded if they don't have a toy their friends already have.

Whereas children are relatively unsophisticated when it comes to adverts, young teens already understand the way advertising works and are often incredibly critical of the adverts that they see.

Marketers admit that this makes them one of the most difficult groups to develop advertising for. While children want to be accepted by peers, teens are also driven by the desire to be part of the 'coolest' group in their school. This means advertisers have to give their products a cachet of cool without being seen as 'trying too hard' (the quality that respondents in teen surveys regard as being beyond the pale).

One of the ways advertisers have got round this is to produce ads that don't look like ads. For instance, print ads or stickers that don't so much sell a product as direct teens to a difficult-to-find website where they can find out more. The idea is to make teens feel that they're part of an exclusive club – and are in on information that peers or parents don't know or understand. In these ways advertisers can use teens' naturally rebellious instincts to sell them expensive products.

KidsAndAdvertising, adapted

Exercise 2: *Why advertisers target children*

1 Write a summary of paragraphs 1–7 (up to the dots) explaining why advertisers target children and how children and their parents respond to such advertising. You should use you own words as far as possible and write about 150 words.

The following questions are on paragraph 8 onwards.

2 Give the meanings of the following words and phrases as used in the passage:

media-saturated	indistinguishable	peer group
proliferation	critically evaluate	cachet
sophistication	animated world	beyond the pale
negotiating		

3 Explain why advertisers make use of cartoon animals in their campaigns and how young children respond to them.

4 Explain what 'pester power' is and how advertisers make use of it.

5 How do young teens differ from younger children in the ways that they respond to advertisements?

6 By referring to the last two paragraphs, explain fully, using your own words, how advertisers attempt to appeal to young teenagers.

Here are some more points to consider about advertisements and the techniques they use.

Different types of advertisements

So far, we have considered mainly advertisements that appear in magazines, newspapers and on television. There are obvious differences between these, perhaps the main one being that television advertisements can use moving images and include sound and spoken dialogue. There is also the possibility of using either real-life actors or animated cartoons to convey the advertiser's message.

With television advertisements in particular, the advertising companies will carefully research the likely audience for different television programmes and take into account the time of day when their advertisement is being transmitted. For example, advertisements for toys and games are most likely to be shown during programmes watched mainly by children or whole families, whereas advertisements for furniture stores are likely to be transmitted when the audience consists mainly of adults. Radio programmes use a similar approach.

Billboards are the large advertisement hoardings that you see by the sides of main roads. Drivers are likely to be passing at speed, so billboards need to convey their message mainly through graphic images as there is not time (nor is it safe) for people in cars to stop and read lengthy text.

Another type of advertisement is a **public information advertisement**, which is usually funded by a government or other official body and aims to raise people's awareness of an issue of national importance. For example, it could be concerned with encouraging healthy eating, warning people of the dangers of smoking or even reminding your parents that they need to pay their income-tax bills by a certain date.

Techniques used by advertisers

Advertisers use tried and trusted techniques to make sure that their audience is aware of their products. These include **celebrity endorsements** – using well-known film stars or sporting personalities to claim that they use the product being advertised. The idea here is that their fans will then buy the product to be like their hero.

Another technique is the use of **slogans** or **jingles**. A slogan is an easily memorable word or phrase chosen to draw your attention to the product being advertised (the word 'slogan' comes from an Old Irish word meaning 'battle cry'). Advertising jingles are catchy tunes and phrases which become associated with a particular product. Very often, the audience may find these jingles intensely irritating but, nevertheless, will be unable to get them (or the product) out of their minds and so the advertisers will have achieved their purpose.

Many advertisements appeal through their use of humour. Others adopt the opposite approach and, in their appearance and tone, initially appear not to be advertisements at all but genuine magazine articles or short television feature films. It is only when the interested readers or viewers reach the end of the feature that they realise what its real purpose is.

What other techniques commonly used by advertisers can you think of?

Activity

Find examples of different types of advertisements and of advertising techniques. Then copy and complete the following table:

Type	Description	Techniques used	Comments (e.g. effectiveness)
Magazine			
Newspaper			
Television			
Radio			
Billboard			
Public information			
Other			

Reading for pleasure

This article is by an advertising copywriter (someone who writes the texts of advertisements) and explains some of the secrets of the trade.

Advertising secrets I learned from the Kirby vacuum cleaner man

BY KARON THACKSTON

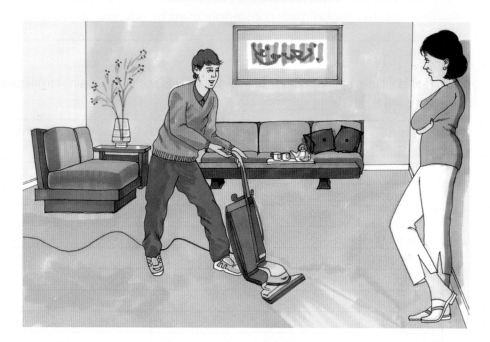

I was just sitting here at my computer (as usual) when my husband walked in and announced, 'There's a man here to see you.' What? I wasn't expecting anyone. 'Who is it,' I asked. 'Some guy who wants to speak with my wife.' Okay, my husband was home so I knew I was safe. I ventured outside to see who it was.

I was promptly met on my porch by a smiling face who presented me with a free box of laundry detergent. This seemingly nice young man told me he was in the neighbourhood and wanted to give me this free gift. Being the sceptic I am, my first thought was, 'Oh yeah … and what kind of sales pitch?'

He proceeded to walk to his truck, then turned and asked if I had a minute. 'Yep, here it comes,' I thought. I said I was a little busy but asked what he wanted. The smile came back to his face as he said, 'I want to make your life easier.'

(Secret 1 – Give your customers something absolutely free of charge. This makes them appreciative and brings about a feeling of goodwill. It can be free useful articles, a free ebook, a sample or trial … anything free.)

He began to pull box after box from the back of his SUV [sport utility vehicle]. As he approached my door, loaded down, he asked if I would allow him to vacuum and clean my carpets … all free, of course. At first I was going to turn him down cold. I wasn't in the vacuum or carpet cleaner buying mood. But then I wondered if I might be able to learn something from this representative of one of the most successful vacuum cleaner companies in America. I decided to give in and allow the demonstration, hoping to glean some 'secrets' I could use in my copywriting.

As he walked into the living room, he began to set up the vacuum. Small talk followed. He complimented me on the interior design of my house, asked what brand of vacuum I used, how I liked it, how old it was, if I had considered buying a new vacuum, if anyone in my family suffered from allergies and how much time I spent cleaning the house.

(Secret 2 – Get to know your customers. By collecting this information, the salesman was mentally tailoring his 'pitch' to suit me. He was making notes to include the elements of his presentation that would appeal to me personally, and leave out those that would not.)

Next, the Kirby man (whom I'll call Roger) began to ask me questions that I would obviously have to say 'yes' to. Roger asked, 'Would you like to be able to spend less time cleaning with better results?' He asked, 'Would you like to know that the allergens AND the dirt are taken out of your upholstery and carpeting?' And finally, he asked, 'Would you like your new carpet to last twice as long?' Needless to say, the answer to all three was 'yes'.

(Secret 3 – Get them in the habit of saying 'yes'. If you get someone in the habit of saying 'yes', they are going to be more likely to agree with you when it comes to other questions, like 'Are you ready to buy a new vacuum?'!)

Roger asked me to get my old vacuum from the closet. I did. He asked me to bring him a box of salt. (Yes, I saw it coming but I did it anyway.) He began to pour the salt onto my carpet. Then (as expected) he ground it in with his foot. He took my old vacuum and asked me to let him know when I thought it had sucked up all the salt. On came the vacuum and the challenge began!

After about fifteen passes, I instructed Roger to stop. He did. Then he reached behind him and rolled over the Kirby G6 – Limited Edition. He opened the latch where the bag goes and placed a black, thin pad over it. Next, he flipped on the 'onboard transmission', put the vacuum into 'drive' and began the first part of his demonstration.

Just six passes later, he stopped the Kirby, opened the bag latch and pulled out the black pad. It was covered with salt! It was also covered with dirt, sand, lint and hair. It was extremely gross, not to mention embarrassing!

(Secret 4 – Prove your point. Just telling someone that your product or service works means nothing. You have to prove that you can and will do what you say. If you can't offer an online demonstration, use testimonials, offer references that tell about before and after results. Or give a free trial period so the customer can check it out themselves.)

'I know you're busy, ma'am, but I just wanted to show you that. I'll finish vacuuming now and then clean your living room,' said Roger. I knew Roger and I weren't finished yet, but I went back to my computer and let him do his work.

Sure enough, about ten minutes later, Roger asked where he would find our trash can. I walked around the corner to see what needed to be thrown away and was immediately horrified! He had used those little pads while vacuuming the entire room! There were disks all over my living room just covered with hair, lint, fibres, dust, sand and who knows what else. The fear of creepy-crawly things in my house started to rise up within me. All this junk was in my carpet? How disgusting! My house wasn't as clean as I thought it was. 'I'm sorry for the mess, ma'am, but we are only allowed to use these demonstration pads to vacuum with. I'll throw them away if you'll show me to your garbage can.'

(Secret 5 – Play on emotion. By leaving all those little demonstration pads around the room, Roger was subtly telling me that my house wasn't very clean. He was reminding me of the initial conversation we had about allergens and getting my house cleaner in less time. It was working, too. I began to think about all the mess deep down inside my carpet, and drapes [curtains], and rugs, and upholstery.)

'Can I try to get these stains out for you?' was the cry from the living room. 'Sure, go ahead,' I replied. Roger continued to work, as did I. A few minutes later he asked if I would come see if the stains were still noticeable. They weren't! I'd tried to get the stains out before but had no luck. 'Good,' Roger smiled, 'I'll clean the rest for you now.'

I continued banging on my keyboard until I heard the whirring of the motor stop. Roger peeked around the corner and told me it would take an hour or so for the carpet to dry enough to walk on. 'Do you mind if I get my gear together in here?' I agreed.

As he was putting up hoses and attachments, he began to explain the extreme versatility of the Kirby G6 – Limited Edition. The package he had with him that day came with a base vacuum which offered an 'onboard transmission' so the motor wouldn't wear out. It also allowed the vacuum to be easier to push. It offered the ability to blow as well as pull suction. This, as Roger explained, was useful for blowing up pool toys or inflatable balls – and for deflating air mattresses, etc., so they would lie completely flat for storage. The carpet cleaner attachment would ... Well, you get the idea.

(Secret 6 – Focus on benefits, not features. We've all heard the phrase before, however most don't apply it. I wouldn't care anything in the world about a vacuum with 'onboard transmission' because I don't have a clue what it is or what it does for me. Once [it's] explained, however, I love the idea of a vacuum that 'drives itself'.)

Lastly, after the full tour of how easy the vacuum was to operate, how much cleaner my house would be with less effort, and how versatile the vacuum/carpet cleaner was ... we got to the price.

Needless to say, with Kirby's reputation, I was expecting to pay an arm and a leg. However, Roger simply said, 'All this can be yours for just $3 per day.' That didn't sound so bad. 'For how many days,' my cynical self asked. Roger laughed and pulled out his pricing sheet. To answer the question that you've had since the beginning of the article ... Yes, I bought the vacuum.

(Secret 7 – Save the price for last. Get them to love your product or service and then – if possible – break the price out into as small an increment as you can. This saves the prospective customer from suffering 'sticker shock' and makes the item appear more affordable.)

Was it worth it? Yes and yes. It was worth my time to find out how one of the most successful vacuum cleaner companies in America does its sales magic; and it was worth the price of the vacuum, too. I learned a lot from the Kirby vacuum cleaner man, and my house looks great!

Writing

Activity

Choose one of the advertisements that you have collected and write a detailed analysis of how it sets out to persuade its audience to buy the product that is being advertised. You should consider the following points:

- What particular social group or groups is the advertisement aimed at and what assumptions, if any, does it make about them? For example, is the advertisement appealing to people's wish to be rich or fashionable?
- What is actually being advertised? What specific feature of the product does the advertisement focus on and why?
- Where and when was the advertisement published and how does this relate to its target audience?
- How is language used in the advertisement and what is its effect? Does the advertisement contain hyperbole – words such as 'miracle', 'sensational', 'magic'? Does it use more aggressive words or phrases such as 'challenge', 'buy now before it's too late', and so on? Remember, advertisements frequently use a direct tone of address: the second-person pronoun 'you' features prominently in many advertisements.
- What images does the advertisement use and why? Does it use stereotypes – for example are women shown doing household chores or men driving fast sports cars?

Group activity

One of the skills of advertising is to make something which is really quite mundane appear attractive and exciting so that people will want to buy it. Working in a group of three or four, imagine that you are a team of advertising agents who have been given the task of promoting your school buildings and grounds as a luxury leisure centre for the public to use for short keep-fit health breaks.

Although you should not tell complete untruths, the skill in this task is to bend the truth sufficiently to make the facilities sound inviting and attractive. For example, you *might* describe the school canteen as an 'on-site restaurant seating over a 100 people in one sitting with the potential for serving gourmet food in unusual and interesting surroundings'. There are, after all, lots of tables and chairs in most school canteens. Many visitors would probably find the paintwork and floor coverings different from what they're used to and all kitchens have the *potential* to cook gourmet food even if they don't usually serve it!

Let your imaginations loose on this task and use whatever ICT facilities you can that will help you to produce the glossiest brochure.

Speaking and listening

> Group activity
>
> As part of the advertising campaign in the previous activity, create a 5-minute radio advertisement, complete with endorsements from satisfied members of the public, that explains what is on offer at the 'leisure centre' at your school. Then present your advertisement to the rest of your class.

Key skills

Figures of speech

Euphemisms

One of the skills of writing advertisements is to make something which is not very interesting, or perhaps, even unpleasant, appear attractive and exciting so that potential customers will want to purchase it. In order to do this, advertising copywriters often take some liberties with language.

For example, think about the range of products now generally known as 'deodorants'. The purpose of a deodorant is to make a person smell attractive and, quite possibly, to hide more unpleasant smells such as dried sweat and so on. However, the advertising team that had to promote the first deodorants to the general public had a problem. A direct address to people saying, 'You smell, but use our product and you'll smell more pleasant' might well offend rather than appeal as most people do not like to be told that they smell! The problem lies in the word 'smell', which has unpleasant connotations. So, the advertisers searched for a word that meant something similar to 'smell' but – at the time – had more positive associations. They came up with the word 'odour'. It was apparently far less offensive to refer to people as having 'body odour' than to say that their bodies had a smell and so the term 'deodorant' was formed.

Disguising an unpleasant or offensive detail by substituting a more agreeable term is known as using a **euphemism**. We often use euphemisms in everyday speech; think, for example, of the terms we commonly use for dying or for death itself, such as 'pass away', 'breathe one's last' or 'eternal rest'. Similarly, clothing manufacturers, among others, will refer to their customers as having 'fuller figures' or as being 'amply built' rather than saying outright that their clothes are designed for people who are fat. Euphemisms are used to describe people who do certain unpleasant jobs: rat catchers, for example, are known as 'rodent operatives'. You might also like to think of the way euphemisms are used in schools – if teachers describe a group of students as being 'challenging',

it is likely that they really mean that these students are very badly behaved!

Euphemisms are part of everyday English expression. It is important that you are aware of their meanings as this will help you to speak and write effective idiomatic English.

Exercise: Euphemisms

1 Here is a list of euphemisms. Try to work out what they mean and where and by whom they are likely to be used.

armed intervention	educationally challenged
between jobs	in reduced circumstances
broad in the beam	negative patient outcome
correctional facility	powder one's nose
economical with the truth	smallest room in the house

2 Teachers sometimes use euphemisms when writing reports on students, especially on those whose behaviour isn't all it should be. In the following report, the euphemistic phrases are in italics. Read it through and then write your own version, saying what you think the teacher really meant.

Joe has *found much of the work challenging* this year and *needs to adopt a more focused approach* to his studies. He is *a lively member of the class* and *always expresses himself confidently and forcefully* whenever he is given the opportunity to do so. However, *he does not always accept authority easily* and, at times, *can be somewhat distracted* during lessons. He has *a good social network of friends and relates well to his peers, with whom he communicates regularly*. In general, he tends *to work better at practical than academic activities* and his work in the latter will improve *once he realises the importance of homework*. He has *a somewhat relaxed attitude to school life* and I suspect that *he is not working to his full potential*.

Food for thought

In general, euphemisms are quite harmless and can be quite entertaining. However, in an essay written in 1946, George Orwell (who also wrote the novel *1984*) came up with the following words of warning which are still relevant to us today. You might like to consider how far you agree with his views.

'Politics and the English Language'

In our time, political speech and writing are largely the defence of the indefensible. Things like ... purges and deportations, the dropping of the atom bombs on Japan, can indeed be defended, but only by arguments which are too brutal for most people to face, and which do not square with the professed aims of the political parties. Thus political language has to consist largely of euphemism, question-begging and sheer cloudy vagueness. Defenceless villages are bombarded from the air, the inhabitants driven out into the countryside, the cattle machine-gunned, the huts set on fire with incendiary bullets: this is called pacification. Millions of peasants are robbed of their farms and sent trudging along the roads with no more than they can carry: this is called transfer of population or rectification of frontiers. People are imprisoned for years without trial, or shot in the back of the neck or sent to die of scurvy in Arctic lumber camps: this is called elimination of unreliable elements. Such phraseology is needed if one wants to name things without calling up mental pictures of them. Consider for instance some [defender of] totalitarianism. He cannot say outright, 'I believe in killing off your opponents when you can get good results by doing so.' Probably, therefore, he will say something like this:

'While freely conceding that the regime exhibits certain features which the humanitarian may be inclined to deplore, we must, I think, agree that a certain curtailment of the right to political opposition is an unavoidable concomitant of transitional periods, and that the rigours which [this regime's] people have been called upon to undergo have been amply justified in the sphere of concrete achievement.'

The inflated style itself is a kind of euphemism. A mass of Latin words falls upon the facts like soft snow, blurring the outline and covering up all the details. The great enemy of clear language is insincerity. When there is a gap between one's real and one's declared aims, one turns as it were instinctively to long words and exhausted idioms, like a cuttlefish spurting out ink. In our age there is no such thing as 'keeping out of politics'. All issues are political issues, and politics itself is a mass of lies, evasions, folly, hatred, and schizophrenia. When the general atmosphere is bad, language must suffer.

George Orwell

6 Detective and ghost stories

Reading

In this chapter we shall be looking at examples of two different types of prose fiction: detective stories and ghost stories. Both are popular forms of writing and possess similar features and qualities. Ghosts have always fascinated people and have been a feature of all forms of imaginative literature for centuries. On the other hand, crime fiction did not really become prominent until the second half of the nineteenth century; *The Murders in the Rue Morgue*, written in 1841 by the American author Edgar Allan Poe, is considered to be one of the earliest and most influential detectives stories. (Poe also wrote stories dealing with supernatural happenings.) However, both genres of fiction depend very much on the building of suspense, on the creation of a sinister and mysterious atmosphere and, very often, on ingenious and cleverly constructed plots.

Detectives

Crime stories depend strongly on complicated plots which very often contain an unexpected twist at the end by which the criminal is finally revealed. Another key feature of these stories is the character of the master detective who is responsible for solving the crimes. In the following extracts we encounter two such characters as they meet their clients. The first extract focuses on the legendary Victorian private detective Sherlock Holmes, from the story 'The Speckled Band', created by Sir Arthur Conan Doyle; the second on the contemporary Botswanian detective Mma Ramotswe, from the *No. 1 Ladies' Detective Agency* book *Tears of the Giraffe* by Alexander McCall Smith.

Read both extracts carefully and then answer the question that follows on page 83.

Sherlock Holmes

'Good morning, madam,' said Holmes cheerily. 'My name is Sherlock Holmes. This is my intimate friend and associate, Dr Watson, before whom you can speak as freely as before myself. Ha! I am glad to see that Mrs Hudson has had the good sense to light the fire. Pray draw up to it, and I shall order you a cup of hot coffee, for I observe that you are shivering.'

'It is not cold which makes me shiver,' said the woman in a low voice, changing her seat as requested.

'What, then?'

"SHE RAISED HER VEIL."

'It is fear, Mr Holmes. It is terror.' She raised her veil as she spoke, and we could see that she was indeed in a pitiable state of agitation, her face all drawn and grey, with restless frightened eyes, like those of some hunted animal. Her features and figure were those of a woman of thirty, but her hair was shot with premature grey, and her expression was weary and haggard. Sherlock Holmes ran her over with one of his quick, all-comprehensive glances.

'You must not fear,' said he soothingly, bending forward and patting her forearm. 'We shall soon set matters right, I have no doubt. You have come in by train this morning, I see.'

'You know me, then?'

'No, but I observe the second half of a return ticket in the palm of your left glove. You must have started early, and yet you had a good drive in a dog-cart, along heavy roads, before you reached the station.'

The lady gave a violent start and stared in bewilderment at my companion.

'There is no mystery, my dear madam,' said he, smiling. 'The left arm of your jacket is spattered with mud in no less than seven places. The marks are perfectly fresh. There is no vehicle save a dog-cart which throws up mud in that way, and then only when you sit on the left-hand side of the driver.'

'Whatever your reasons may be, you are perfectly correct,' said she. 'I started from home before six, reached Leatherhead at twenty past, and came in by the first train to Waterloo. Sir, I can stand this strain no longer; I shall go mad if it continues. I have no one to turn to – none, save only one, who cares for me, and he, poor fellow, can be of little aid. I have heard of you, Mr Holmes; I have heard of you from Mrs Farintosh, whom you helped in the hour of her sore need. It was from her that I had your address. Oh, sir, do you not think that you could help me, too, and at least throw a little light through the dense darkness which surrounds me? At present it is out of my power to reward you for your services, but in a month or six weeks I shall be married, with the control of my own income, and then at least you shall not find me ungrateful.'

Holmes turned to his desk and, unlocking it, drew out a small case-book, which he consulted.

'Farintosh,' said he. 'Ah yes, I recall the case; it was concerned with an opal tiara. I think it was before your time, Watson. I can only say, madam, that I shall be happy to devote the same care to your case as I did to that of your friend. As to reward, my profession is its own reward; but you are at liberty to defray whatever expenses I may be put to, at the time which suits you best. And now I beg that you will lay before us everything that may help us in forming an opinion upon the matter.'

Sir Arthur Conan Doyle

Mma Ramotswe

The woman took her hand, correctly, Mma Ramotswe noticed, in the proper Botswana way, placing her left hand on her right forearm as a mark of respect. Most white people shook hands very rudely, snatching just one hand and leaving their other hand free to perform all sorts of mischief. This woman had at least learned something about how to behave.

She invited the caller to sit down in the chair which they kept for clients, while Mma Makutsi busied herself with the kettle.

'I'm Mrs Andrea Curtin,' said the visitor. 'I heard from somebody in my embassy that you were a detective and you might be able to help me.'

Mma Ramotswe raised an eyebrow. 'Embassy?'

'The American Embassy,' said Mrs Curtin. 'I asked them to give me the name of a detective agency.'

Mma Ramotswe smiled. 'I am glad that they recommended me,' she said. 'But what do you need?'

The woman had folded her hands on her lap and now she looked down at them. The skin of her hands was mottled, Mma Ramotswe noticed, in the way that white people's hands were if they were exposed to too much sun. Perhaps she was an American who had lived for many years in Africa; there were many of these people. They grew to love Africa and they stayed, sometimes until they died. Mma Ramotswe could understand why they did this. She could not imagine why anybody would want to live anywhere else. How did people survive in cold, northern climates, with all that snow and rain and darkness?

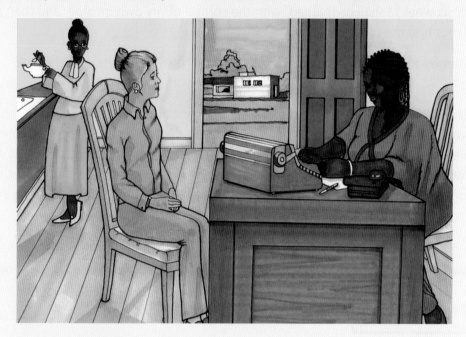

'I could say that I am looking for somebody,' said Mrs Curtin, raising her eyes to meet Mma Ramotswe's gaze. 'But then that would suggest that there is somebody to look for. I don't think that there is so I suppose I should say that I'm trying to find out what happened to somebody, quite a long time ago. I don't expect that that person is alive. In fact, I am certain that he is not. But I want to find out what happened.'

Mma Ramotswe nodded. 'Sometimes it is important to know,' she said. 'And I am sorry, Mma, if you have lost somebody.'

Mrs Curtin smiled. 'You're very kind. Yes, I lost somebody.'

'When was this?' asked Mma Ramotswe.

'Ten years ago,' said Mrs Curtin. 'Ten years ago I lost my son.'

For a few moments there was a silence. Mma Ramotswe glanced over to where Mma Makutsi was standing near the sink and noticed that her secretary was watching Mrs Curtin attentively. When she caught her employer's gaze, Mma Makutsi looked guilty and returned to her task of filling the teapot.

Mma Ramotswe broke the silence. 'I am very sorry. I know what it is like to lose a child.'

'Do you, Mma?'

She was not sure whether the question had an edge to it, as if it were a challenge, but she answered gently. 'I lost my baby. He did not live.'

Mrs Curtin lowered her gaze. 'Then you know,' she said. Mma Makutsi had now prepared the bush tea and she brought over a chipped enamel tray on which two mugs were standing. Mrs Curtin took hers gratefully, and began to sip on the hot, red liquid.

'I should tell you something about myself,' said Mrs Curtin. 'Then you will know why I am here and why I would like you to help me. If you can help me I shall be very pleased, but if not, I shall understand.'

'I will tell you,' said Mma Ramotswe. 'I cannot help everybody. I will not waste our time or your money. I shall tell you whether I can help.'

Alexander McCall Smith

Exercise 1: Sherlock Holmes and Mma Ramotswe

Both of these extracts are from the beginning of the story. Write a detailed comparison of the two passages. Be sure to refer closely to the passages in your answer. You should focus on:

- the similarities and differences between the characters of Sherlock Holmes and Mma Ramotswe, in particular how they behave and the ways in which they treat their clients
- the settings in which the scenes take place
- the ways in which the writers introduce events and how you think that the stories may develop.

Ghosts

The next passage is from *The Woman in Black*, by the contemporary writer Susan Hill. In this story, a young solicitor is spending the night in an empty house in a deserted part of the English countryside, where he has been sent to go through the papers of the deceased owner. He has a dog, Spider, for company. He has just been woken by a mysterious noise.

Read the passage carefully and answer the questions that follow.

The Woman in Black

And then, from somewhere within the depths of the house but somewhere not very far from the room in which I was I heard a noise. It was a faint noise, and, strain my ears as I might, I could not make out exactly what it was. It was a sound like a regular yet intermittent bump or rumble. Nothing else happened. There were no footsteps, no creaking floorboards, the air was absolutely still, the wind did not moan through the casement. Only the muffled noise went on and the dog continued to stand, bristling at the door, now putting her nose to the gap at the bottom and snuffling along, now taking a pace backwards, head cocked and, like me, listening, listening. And, every so often, she growled again.

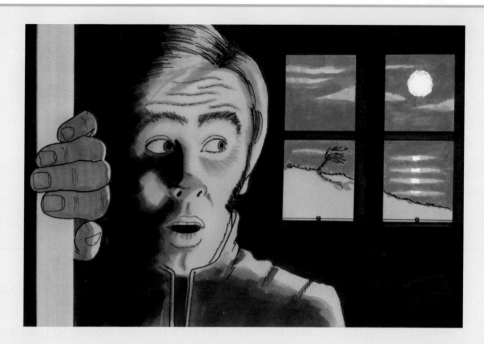

In the end, I suppose because nothing else happened and because I did have the dog to take with me, I managed to get out of bed, though I was shaken and my heart beat uncomfortably fast within me. But it took some time for me to find sufficient reserves of courage to enable me to open the bedroom door and stand out in the dark corridor. The moment I did so, Spider shot ahead and I heard her padding about, sniffing intently at every closed door, still growling and grumbling down in her throat.

After a while, I heard the odd sound again. It seemed to be coming from along the passage to my left, at the far end. But it was still quite impossible to identify. Very cautiously, listening, hardly breathing, I ventured a few steps in that direction. Spider went ahead of me. The passage led only to three other bedrooms on either side and, one by one, regaining my nerve as I went, I opened them and looked inside each one. Nothing, only heavy old furniture and empty unmade beds and, in the rooms at the back of the house, moonlight. Down below me on the ground floor of the house, silence, a seething, blanketing, almost tangible silence, and a musty darkness, thick as felt.

And then I reached the door at the very end of the passage. Spider was there before me and her body, as she sniffed beneath it, went rigid, her growling grew louder. I put my hand on her collar, stroked the rough, short hair, as much for my own reassurance as for hers. I could feel the tension in her limbs and body and it answered to my own.

This was the door without a keyhole, which I had been unable to open on my first visit to Eel Marsh House. I had no idea what was beyond it. Except the sound. It was coming from within that room, not very loud but just to hand, on the other side of that single wooden partition. It was a sound of something bumping gently on the floor, in a rhythmic sort of way, a familiar sort of sound and yet one I still could not exactly place, a sound that seemed to belong to my past, to waken old, half-forgotten memories and associations deep within me, a sound that, in any other place, would not have made me afraid but would, I thought, have been curiously comforting, friendly.

But, at my feet, the dog Spider began to whine, a thin, pitiful, frightened moan, and to back away from the door a little and press against my legs. My throat felt constricted and dry and I had begun to shiver. There was something in that room and I could not get to it, nor would I dare to, if I were able: I told myself it was a rat or a trapped bird, fallen down the chimney into the hearth and unable to get out again. But the sound was not that of some small, panic-stricken creature. Bump bump. Pause. Bump bump. Pause. Bump bump. Bump bump. Bump bump.

I think that I might have stood there, in bewilderment and terror, all night, or else taken to my heels, with the dog, and run out of the house altogether, had I not heard another, faint sound. It came from behind me, not directly behind but from the front of the house. I turned away from the locked door and went back, shakily, groping along the wall to my bedroom, guided by the slant of moonlight that reached out into the darkness of the corridor. The dog was half a pace ahead of me.

There was nothing in the room at all, the bed was as I had left it, there had been no disturbances; then I realised that the sounds had been coming not from within the room but outside it, beyond the window. I pulled it up as far as the sash would allow and looked out. There lay the marshes, silver-grey and empty, there was the water of the estuary, flat as a mirror with the full moon lying upturned upon it. Nothing. No one. Except, like a wash from far, far away, so that I half wondered if I were remembering and reliving the memory, a cry, a child's cry. But no. The slightest of breezes stirred the surface of the water, wrinkling it, and passing dryly through the reed beds and away. Nothing more.

Susan Hill

Exercise 2: The Woman in Black

1 Write a summary of this passage in which you explain:
- what the narrator saw and heard
- what the narrator's thoughts and feelings were
- what Spider, the dog, did.

You should write about 250 words and use your own words as far as possible.
2 Compare your summarised version with the original passage. What has been lost by just concentrating on the facts contained in the original?
3 Explain fully, with close reference to the original passage, how the author's description of the house and the events that happen helps to create suspense in the reader's mind.

Now, here is a complete ghost story. Its title is simply 'A Ghost Story' and it is by the American writer Mark Twain (real name Samuel Langhorne Clemens). Mark Twain lived in the nineteenth century, from 1835 to 1910, and this story was published in 1903. The story is divided into three sections with exercises following each section, but as it develops to a slightly unexpected ending, try to resist the temptation to jump to the last page to see what happens!

Read the first section carefully and then answer the questions that follow on pages 87–88.

'A Ghost Story' – Part 1

I took a large room, far up Broadway, in a huge old building whose upper storeys had been wholly unoccupied for years until I came. The place had long been given up to dust and cobwebs, to solitude and silence. I seemed to be groping among the tombs and invading the privacy of the dead, that first night I climbed up to my quarters. For the first time in my life a superstitious dread came over me; and as I turned a dark angle of the stairway and an invisible cobweb swung its sleazy woof in my face and clung there, I shuddered as one who had encountered a phantom.

I was glad enough when I reached my room and locked out the mould and the darkness. A cheery fire was burning in the grate, and I sat down before it with a comforting sense of relief. For two hours I sat there, thinking of bygone times; recalling old scenes, and summoning half-forgotten faces out of the mists of the past; listening, in fancy, to voices that long ago grew silent for all time, and to once familiar songs that nobody sings now. And as my reverie softened down to a sadder and sadder pathos, the shrieking of the winds outside softened to a wail, the angry beating of the rain against the panes diminished to a tranquil patter, and one by one the noises in the street subsided, until the hurrying footsteps of the last belated straggler died away in the distance and left no sound behind.

The fire had burned low. A sense of loneliness crept over me. I arose and undressed, moving on tiptoe about the room, doing stealthily what I had to do, as if I were environed by sleeping enemies whose slumbers it would be fatal to break. I covered up in bed, and lay listening to the rain and wind and the faint creaking of distant shutters, till they lulled me to sleep.

I slept profoundly, but how long I do not know. All at once I found myself awake, and filled with a shuddering expectancy. All was still. All but my own heart – I could hear it beat. Presently the bedclothes began to slip away slowly toward the foot of the bed, as if someone were pulling them! I could not stir; I could not speak. Still the blankets slipped deliberately away, till my breast was uncovered. Then with a great effort I seized them and drew them over my head. I waited, listened, waited. Once more that steady pull began, and once more I lay torpid a century of dragging seconds till my breast was naked again. At last I roused my energies and snatched the covers back to their place and held them with a strong grip. I waited. By and by I felt a faint tug, and took a fresh grip. The tug strengthened to a steady strain – it grew stronger and stronger. My hold parted, and for the third time the blankets slid away. I groaned. An answering groan came from the foot of the bed! Beaded drops of sweat stood upon my forehead. I was more dead than alive. Presently I heard a heavy footstep in my room – the step of an elephant, it seemed to me – it was not like anything human. But it was moving from me – there was relief in that. I heard it approach the door – pass out without moving bolt or lock – and wander away among the dismal corridors, straining the floors and joists till they creaked again as it passed – and then silence reigned once more.

When my excitement had calmed, I said to myself, 'This is a dream – simply a hideous dream.' And so I lay thinking it over until I convinced myself that it was a dream, and then a comforting laugh relaxed my lips and I was happy again. I got up and struck a light; and when I found that the locks and bolts were just as I had left them, another soothing laugh welled in my heart and rippled from my lips. I took my pipe and lit it, and was just sitting down before the fire, when – down went the pipe out of my nerveless fingers, the blood forsook my cheeks, and my placid breathing was cut short with a gasp! In the ashes on the hearth, side by side with my own bare footprint, was another, so vast that in comparison mine was but an infant's! Then I had had a visitor, and the elephant tread was explained.

Mark Twain

Exercise 3: 'A Ghost Story' – Part 1

1 Explain, using your own words, the following words and phrases as used in the passage:

solitude	belated straggler
sleazy woof	environed
reverie	torpid
pathos	century

2 Give three details from paragraph 1 that tell you that the narrator feels uneasy in his new lodgings and explain why you have chosen them.

3 What makes the narrator feel more comfortable once he reaches his room?

4 How does the narrator pass the time in his room before going to bed?

5 Explain fully, using details from the passage, the narrator's state of mind while he is sitting in his room.

6 Look closely at paragraphs 2 and 3 and explain how the descriptions of the room and the world outside the room help to reinforce the narrator's mood.

7 Explain, using your own words, what the narrator experiences when he wakes up from his profound sleep in paragraph 4.

8 What impression do you receive of the character of the narrator from this opening section of the story? Do you think that he appears to be a well-balanced person? Consider the tone of voice of his narrative.

9 How far does your impression of the narrator's character help you to believe in the events that he is describing? Give reasons for your answer.

10 Think about the atmosphere and setting created by the writer – how effective do you find it for the events that are described?

Now read carefully the next section of the story and then answer the questions that follow on pages 89–90.

'A Ghost Story' – Part 2

I put out the light and returned to bed, palsied with fear. I lay a long time, peering into the darkness, and listening. – Then I heard a grating noise overhead, like the dragging of a heavy body across the floor; then the throwing down of the body, and the shaking of my windows in response to the concussion. In distant parts of the building I heard the muffled slamming of doors. I heard, at intervals, stealthy footsteps creeping in and out among the corridors, and up and down the stairs. Sometimes these noises approached my door, hesitated, and went away again. I heard the clanking of chains faintly, in remote passages, and listened while the clanking grew nearer – while it wearily climbed the stairways, marking each move by the loose surplus of chain that fell with an accented rattle upon each

succeeding step as the goblin that bore it advanced. I heard muttered sentences; half-uttered screams that seemed smothered violently; and the swish of invisible garments, the rush of invisible wings. Then I became conscious that my chamber was invaded – that I was not alone. I heard sighs and breathings about my bed, and mysterious whisperings. Three little spheres of soft phosphorescent light appeared on the ceiling directly over my head, clung and glowed there a moment, and then dropped – two of them upon my face and one upon the pillow. They spattered, liquidly, and felt warm. Intuition told me they had turned to gouts of blood as they fell – I needed no light to satisfy myself of that. Then I saw pallid faces, dimly luminous, and white uplifted hands, floating bodiless in the air – floating a moment and then disappearing. The whispering ceased, and the voices and the sounds, and a solemn stillness followed. I waited and listened. I felt that I must have light or die. I was weak with fear. I slowly raised myself toward a sitting posture, and my face came in contact with a clammy hand! All strength went from me apparently, and I fell back like a stricken invalid. Then I heard the rustle of a garment; it seemed to pass to the door and go out.

When everything was still once more, I crept out of bed, sick and feeble, and lit the gas with a hand that trembled as if it were aged with a hundred years. The light brought some little cheer to my spirits. I sat down and fell into a dreamy contemplation of that great footprint in the ashes. By and by its outlines began to waver and grow dim. I glanced up and the broad gas-flame was slowly wilting away. In the same moment I heard that elephantine tread again. I noted its approach, nearer and nearer, along the musty halls, and dimmer and dimmer the light waned. The tread reached my very door and paused – the light had dwindled to a sickly blue, and all things about me lay in a spectral twilight. The door did not open, and yet I felt a faint gust of air fan my cheek, and presently was conscious of a huge, cloudy presence before me. I watched it with fascinated eyes. A pale glow stole over the Thing; gradually its cloudy folds took shape – an arm appeared, then legs, then a body, and last a great sad face looked out of the vapour. Stripped of its filmy housings, naked, muscular and comely, the majestic Cardiff Giant loomed above me!

Mark Twain

Exercise 4: 'A Ghost Story' – Part 2

1 Explain, using your own words, the following words and phrases as used in the passage:

palsied	dimly luminous
concussion	dreamy contemplation
accented rattle	spectral twilight

2 Write a summary of all the ghostly happenings that the narrator experiences in this section and of his thoughts and feelings during this time. You should write about 180 words and use your own words as far as possible.

3 How far do you think the writer deliberately uses ghost-story clichés in his description of the haunting in this section? Identify these clichés and explain as fully as you can what effects they will have on the responses of readers.

Now read carefully the final section of the story and then answer the questions that follow on pages 92–93.

'A Ghost Story' – Part 3

All my misery vanished – for a child might know that no harm could come with that benignant countenance. My cheerful spirits returned at once, and in sympathy with them the gas flamed up brightly again. Never a lonely outcast was so glad to welcome company as I was to greet the friendly giant. I said:

'Why, is it nobody but you? Do you know, I have been scared to death for the last two or three hours? I am most honestly glad to see you. I wish I had a chair – Here, here, don't try to sit down in that thing!'

But it was too late. He was in it before I could stop him and down he went – I never saw a chair shivered so in my life.

'Stop, stop, you'll ruin ev–'

Too late again. There was another crash, and another chair was resolved into its original elements.

'Confound it, haven't you got any judgment at all? Do you want to ruin all the furniture on the place? Here, here, you petrified fool –'

But it was no use. Before I could arrest him he had sat down on the bed, and it was a melancholy ruin.

'Now what sort of a way is that to do? First you come lumbering about the place bringing a legion of vagabond goblins along with you to worry me to death, and then when I overlook an indelicacy of costume which would not be tolerated anywhere by cultivated people except in a respectable theatre, and not even there if the nudity were of your sex, you repay me by wrecking all the furniture you can find to sit down on. And why will you? You damage yourself as much as you do me. You have broken off the end of your spinal column, and littered up the floor with chips of your hams till the place looks like a marble yard. You ought to be ashamed of yourself – you are big enough to know better.'

'Well, I will not break any more furniture. But what am I to do? I have not had a chance to sit down for a century.' And the tears came into his eyes.

'Poor devil,' I said, 'I should not have been so harsh with you. And you are an orphan, too, no doubt. But sit down on the floor here – nothing else can stand your weight – and besides, we cannot be sociable with you away up there above me; I want you down where I can perch on this high counting-house stool and gossip with you face to face.' So he sat down on the floor, and lit a pipe which I gave him, threw one of my red blankets over his shoulders, inverted my sitz-bath on his head, helmet fashion, and made himself picturesque and comfortable. Then he crossed his ankles, while I renewed the fire, and exposed the flat, honeycombed bottoms of his prodigious feet to the grateful warmth.

'What is the matter with the bottom of your feet and the back of your legs, that they are gouged up so?'

'Infernal chilblains – I caught them clear up to the back of my head, roosting out there under Newell's farm. But I love the place; I love it as one loves his old home. There is no peace for me like the peace I feel when I am there.'

We talked along for half an hour, and then I noticed that he looked tired, and spoke of it.

'Tired?' he said. 'Well, I should think so. And now I will tell you all about it, since you have treated me so well. I am the spirit of the Petrified Man that lies across the street there in the museum. I am the ghost of the Cardiff Giant. I can have no rest, no peace, till they have given that poor body burial again. Now what was the most natural thing for me to do, to make men satisfy this wish? Terrify them into it! Haunt the place where the body lay! So I haunted the museum night after night. I even got other spirits to help me. But it did no good, for nobody ever came to the museum at midnight. Then it occurred to me to come over the way and haunt this place a little. I felt that if I ever got a hearing I must succeed, for I had the most efficient company that perdition could furnish. Night after night we have shivered around through these mildewed halls, dragging chains, groaning, whispering, tramping up and down stairs, till, to tell you the truth, I am almost worn out. But when I saw a light in your room tonight I roused my energies again and went at it with a deal of the old freshness. But I am tired out – entirely fagged out. Give me, I beseech you, give me some hope!' I lit off my perch in a burst of excitement, and exclaimed:

|||➡

'This transcends everything! Everything that ever did occur! Why you poor blundering old fossil, you have had all your trouble for nothing – you have been haunting a plaster cast of yourself – the real Cardiff Giant is in Albany! Confound it, don't you know your own remains?'

[Note by Mark Twain: A fact. The original fraud was ingeniously and fraudfully duplicated, and exhibited in New York as the 'only genuine' Cardiff Giant (to the unspeakable disgust of the owners of the real colossus) at the very same time that the latter was drawing crowds at a museum in Albany.]

I never saw such an eloquent look of shame, of pitiable humiliation, overspread a countenance before.

The Petrified Man rose slowly to his feet, and said:

'Honestly, is that true?'

'As true as I am sitting here.'

He took the pipe from his mouth and laid it on the mantel, then stood irresolute a moment (unconsciously, from old habit, thrusting his hands where his pantaloons pockets should have been, and meditatively dropping his chin on his breast); and finally said:

'Well – I never felt so absurd before. The Petrified Man has sold everybody else, and now the mean fraud has ended by selling its own ghost! My son, if there is any charity left in your heart for a poor friendless phantom like me, don't let this get out. Think how you would feel if you had made such an ass of yourself.'

I heard his stately tramp die away, step by step down the stairs and out into the deserted street, and felt sorry that he was gone, poor fellow – and sorrier still that he had carried off my red blanket and my bathtub.

Mark Twain

For details of the story of the Cardiff Giant, see the Reading for pleasure section that follows on pages 93–94.

Exercise 5: 'A Ghost Story' – Part 3

1 Explain, using your own words, the following words and phrases as used in the passage:

benignant countenance	beseech
prodigious	transcends
perdition	meditatively
fagged out	

2 Why do the narrator's 'cheerful spirits' return when he meets the ghost in person?

3 Explain fully, using your own words, what happens when the ghost tries to make himself at home in the narrator's room.

4 Why does the narrator feel pity for the ghost?

5 Explain who the ghost is, why he decided to haunt the museum and how he set about doing it.

6 Explain fully, using your own words, what happens at the end of the story (from the paragraph beginning 'This transcends everything ...' to the end).

7 In what ways does the language used by the writer and the tone of the narrative in this closing section of the story contrast with the earlier sections? How far does this change convey the author's intentions and affect your response to the story?

8 Write a review of the story explaining fully what you liked and disliked about it and giving reasons why you would (or would not) recommend it to your friends.

Reading for pleasure

Mark Twain's 'A Ghost Story' refers to an actual historical event. Here is an account of the Cardiff Giant mystery.

The Cardiff Giant

Date: 1869

The Cardiff Giant, a gigantic stone man 3 m tall, emerged out of the ground and into American life on 16 October 1869, when he was discovered by some workers digging a well behind the barn of William C. 'Stub' Newell in Cardiff, New York. Word of his presence quickly spread, and soon thousands of people were making the journey out to Stub Newell's farm to see the colossus. Even when Newell began charging 50 cents a head to have a look at it, people still kept coming.

Speculation ran rampant over what the giant might be. The central debate was between those who thought it was a petrified man and those who believed

The Cardiff Giant being brought to the surface in 1869

it to be an ancient statue. The 'petrifactionists' theorised that it was one of the giants mentioned in the Bible, where it says, 'There were giants in the earth in those days.'

The truth was somewhat more prosaic. It was actually the creation of an enterprising New York tobacconist named George Hull. The idea of burying a stone giant in the ground occurred to him after he got into an argument with a priest about whether the Bible should be taken literally. Hull, an atheist, didn't think it should. But the priest disagreed and insisted that even the passage where it says 'There were giants in the earth in those days' should be read as a literal fact. According to Hull, after this discussion he immediately 'thought of making a stone, and passing it off as a petrified man'. He figured he could use the fake giant not only to poke fun at people like the priest, but also make some money.

Hull's idea turned out to be a stroke of genius. The entire venture cost him over $2600 (all done with the collusion of the farmer Newell and the stonecutters who carved the giant), but the gamble paid off when a group of businessmen paid $37 500 to buy the giant and move it to Syracuse (a town in New York State), where it could be more prominently exhibited.

In Syracuse the giant came under closer scrutiny. Othniel C. Marsh, a palaeontologist from Yale University, paid it a visit and declared it to be a clumsy fake. He pointed out that chisel marks were still plainly visible on it. These should have worn away if the giant had been in the ground for any appreciable length of time. Sensing that the game was up (and having already cashed in), Hull confessed. But the public didn't seem to care that it was fake. They kept coming to see it anyway. They even began referring to it affectionately as 'Old Hoaxey'.

Recognising the giant's popularity, the great showman P.T. Barnum offered the new owners $60 000 for a three-month lease of it. When his offer was refused, he paid an artist to build an exact plaster replica, which he then put on display in his museum in New York City. Soon the replica was drawing larger crowds than the original. This competition prompted the owners of the giant to file a lawsuit against Barnum, but the judge refused to hear their case unless the 'genuineness' of the original could be proven. Sheepishly they dropped their charges. What is believed to be Barnum's replica of the giant is currently on display in Marvin's Marvelous Mechanical Museum, located outside Detroit.

Many have declared the Cardiff Giant to be the greatest hoax of all time. Whether or not this is the case, its huge size and mysterious presence certainly tapped into some strange element of the post-Civil War American psyche. Although the massive public interest in the giant gradually died down, it remained popular. Even today people still make the journey to visit it at its permanent home in the Farmer's Museum in Cooperstown, New York (down the road from the Baseball Hall of Fame).

Writing

> ## Activity
>
> Write the opening pages of a detective or ghost story (or openings for each if you're feeling inspired) in which you set the scene and introduce the main character(s).
> You should not aim to complete the whole story but should concentrate on creating a suitably convincing and mysterious scenario.

Speaking and listening

> ## Paired activity
>
> Working with a friend, decide on a title for a brief anecdote that, between you, you will relate to the class. However, each of you will know only half of the story. One of you should prepare an account of what actually happened while the other prepares details of the place in which the event took place and the people involved. Toss a coin to decide which of you will start to tell the story. The first story-teller should begin and then, at a suitable point, pause to allow their partner to continue. Carry on taking turns until the account is finished. (The skill required here is that each of you will need to adapt your version of events to match up with your partner's!)

Key skills

Vocabulary

Synonyms

In *Student's Book 2* we looked at how different languages throughout history have influenced the development of English and contributed to modern English vocabulary. One of the languages that has given a large number of words to English is Latin – the language spoken by the Romans 2000 years ago. However, many Latin-derived words did not enter English during the Roman occupation of Britain, which began in the days of the Emperor Claudius. These words became part of the language over 1000 years later during the historical period known as the Renaissance, when the revival of classical learning affected much of Europe. Legal and official documents at this time were written in Latin, which was the common language understood by educated people in different countries.

The English language absorbed these Latinate words and accommodated them alongside English words that already existed which had similar meanings. However, over the centuries, many Latin-derived words have acquired more formal and official associations than the equivalent words derived from Old English. For example, the adjective *cordial* comes from the Latin word *cor*, which means *heart*. The word *heart* itself, which gives us the adjective *hearty*, derives from the Old English word *heort*. In Modern English we can say that someone was given *a hearty welcome* and also that a person received *a cordial welcome*. However, although *hearty* and *cordial* have roots with a common meaning, their associations imply a difference in warmth between the two types of welcome – a *hearty* welcome suggests a very warm and friendly reception with the visitor being welcomed with open arms by all present, whereas a *cordial* one suggests that, although perfectly friendly, the welcome consisted of little more than a polite handshake and, perhaps, the offer of a cup of tea! Being aware of such shades of meaning is a key skill in expressing yourself precisely in written and spoken English.

Exercise: Synonyms

Here are some pairs of synonyms. Use each word in a sentence of its own to illustrate the particular shades of meaning of the pairs. (The Latin-derived word is the first of each pair.)

amicable/friendly	maternal/motherly
antique/old	masculine/manly
cogitation/thought	paternal/fatherly
fraternal/brotherly	science/knowledge
fortuitous/lucky	veracious/truthful

An introduction to Shakespeare

Reading

In *Student's Books 1–3*, we have looked at extracts from the work of authors and poets from around the world and from different periods of history. Each of these writers possesses qualities that make them unique but also qualities that they all share. One of these, of course, is their genius in using the English language. Another, also shared by great painters, musicians and artists in all genres, is their ability to present their audiences with universal truths through their works and to show a profound and perceptive understanding of human nature, regardless of the time or place in which their works were created. Great literature is, in the words of the poet Ezra Pound, 'News that stays news'.

Of all the writers who have written in English over the last 1000 years, the one who is generally considered to be the greatest of them all is the poet and dramatist William Shakespeare (1564–1616). So it is appropriate to devote this chapter to an introduction to his work. Shakespeare's plays and poetry will almost certainly become a feature of your study of English at IGCSE® level and beyond and will provide you with continual rewarding experiences for the remainder of your life.

From a Royal Shakespeare Company production of *Hamlet*

Before we look at an extract from one of his plays, here is some background information that will help you to understand it.

Who was Shakespeare?

Shakespeare was born in the Warwickshire town of Stratford upon Avon. His date of birth is generally considered to have been 23 April 1564 and it is believed that he died, also in Stratford, on his birthday in 1616. For someone so famous whose works are so well known, the precise details of his life are somewhat limited. We know that he was at school in Stratford and that his father was a merchant in the town (and later was awarded his own coat of arms, which was a sign of status). We know that Shakespeare did not attend university, that he married a woman called Anne Hathaway who came from a village near Stratford and who was seven years older than him. They had three children but the direct line of Shakespeare's descendants died out after two generations.

Shakespeare, however, did not spend all his life in Stratford. At some point during the 1590s he moved to London (leaving his wife and family in Stratford) and became involved in the theatrical scene that was taking off in the capital. He worked as an actor in one of the theatre companies, The Lord Chamberlain's Men, and increasingly as a dramatist writing plays for them. We also know that Shakespeare was a part-owner and administrator of this company, which performed at their own theatre, the Globe, on the South Bank of the River Thames. After the accession of James I to the throne of England in 1603, the king became a patron of the company and as a result their name was changed to The King's Men. The fact that the company received the king's patronage indicates their high status and Shakespeare was apparently successful as a theatrical businessman as well as a dramatist and poet.

Although Shakespeare spent most of his adulthood in the exciting world of the London theatre, he still kept his links with Stratford and his family. When he semi-retired from the life of the theatre he returned to Stratford for his last years.

Historical background

The age in which Shakespeare lived was one of great changes. Queen Elizabeth I had provided England with some form of political stability after many years of civil war and upheaval; as well as this England was becoming an important political force within Europe. The Elizabethan period marked the transition from the Middle Ages to Modern Times and it was a time when many important scientific discoveries were being made. The printing press had been invented in England by William Caxton less than a hundred years before Shakespeare was born and this meant that for the first time the world's knowledge was becoming available to all people who were able to read. Shakespeare's generation was one of the first to make use of this opportunity. Travel and communication between countries were becoming increasingly common and a large city such as London would have been home to a cosmopolitan mix of people.

This was also a period in which the arts, and literature in particular, were flourishing. This was partly as a result of changes taking place in the language spoken and written in England, which allowed authors the opportunity to experiment in their writing. The rigid social structure of the medieval period was also breaking up and being replaced by a much more fluid mix of social classes.

The theatre in Shakespeare's time

The commercial theatre in London developed swiftly during the final decades of the sixteenth century. It provided a new, and inexpensive, source of entertainment for all groups of society. Different theatrical companies were established (in most cases supported and financed by important political figures or members of Queen Elizabeth's court) and theatres were built on the outskirts of the city. At this time, theatres and those associated with them were not considered to be fully respectable, and theatres were not allowed to be built within the City of London itself – a rule that almost certainly added to their appeal!

Visiting these public theatres to watch the plays performed there soon became a popular pastime for the people of London. As the theatres were in the open air (and because there was no effective means of artificial lighting) plays were performed during daylight hours. The theatre buildings were circular and the acting area consisted of three sections. The main action took place on an apron stage which thrust out into the audience, who would be situated on three sides of it. At the back of this apron stage was an inner stage that could be used for indoor scenes and

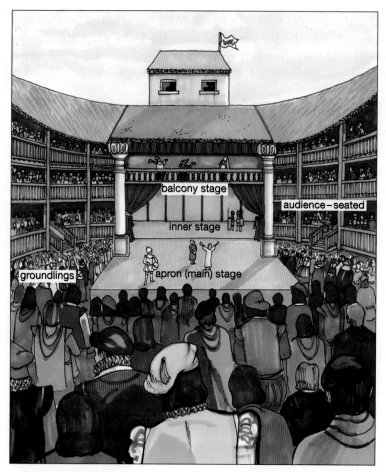

A typical Elizabethan theatre

which could be closed off from the audience's view by curtains. Above the inner stage was a balcony stage which could be used to represent scenes taking place on a castle's battlements, for example.

The actors performed more or less in contemporary Elizabethan costumes (no matter what period of time the play was set in) although some costume concessions were made: kings wore crowns and ghosts had their own distinct appearance. Special effects were very limited and all the parts were played by men or boys, because the theatre was not considered a suitable place for women to perform in. The actors, however, prided themselves as swordsmen and sword fights were an exciting feature of the plays. Actors wore concealed pouches containing animal blood so that they could bleed convincingly when stabbed!

The audience

The audience for the plays represented the complete range of Elizabethan society. The courtiers and nobles wanted to ensure that their investment in the theatre had been well spent and they also expected the plays to contain sufficient verbal wit and philosophical ideas to satisfy their own intellectual interests. In some cases, particularly important members of

A sword fight would help to keep the groundlings entertained.

the aristocracy would have their chairs positioned on the stage itself and the actors would have to act round them. The main seating area in the theatre was occupied by members of the respectable Elizabethan middle class, the merchants, tradesmen and city councillors, who expected a good, exciting story in which right triumphed over wrong.

Finally, the rowdiest and potentially most difficult members of the audience were the groundlings – so called because they occupied the open space in front of the stage and spent their whole time standing up or walking around while they watched the play. These theatre-goers consisted mainly of young apprentices who were out to be entertained and to let off steam. It was, of course, crucial that the plays kept the groundlings engaged as their closeness to the stage and the actors meant that they could cause considerable disruption if they became bored!

This brief survey of the original audience for Shakespeare's plays shows that there was a very wide range of interests to engage. One of the reasons for Shakespeare's enduring appeal is that performances of his plays can still interest and engage a wide range of audiences. This is a result of his close knowledge of what would and would not work on stage, gained from being closely involved with all aspects of theatrical performance.

Shakespeare's plays and their language

At least 37 of the plays written by Shakespeare are still in existence; we do not know if he wrote others that have not survived the passage of time. In his day the texts of plays were not printed as soon as they were written – there were no copyright laws and the theatre companies did not want their exclusive productions to get into the hands of rival companies. It is also possible that dramatists collaborated on some plays. For example, a thirty-eighth play, *Two Noble Kinsmen*, is sometimes attributed to Shakespeare although it is probable that if Shakespeare was involved it was in collaboration with another dramatist, John Fletcher.

Shakespeare's plays can be categorised as three main types: Histories, Comedies and Tragedies:

- The Histories deal with the lives of earlier English kings and include *Richard II* and *Henry V*.
- The Comedies include such plays as *A Midsummer Night's Dream* and *Twelfth Night*.
- The Tragedies (considered by many critics to be Shakespeare's greatest achievements) include *Hamlet*, *Macbeth* and *King Lear*.

Like most other dramatists of his time, Shakespeare wrote his plays in verse (although he also used prose for speeches by some of the less important characters). Technically, the plays are written in what is known as **blank verse** or unrhymed iambic pentameters. A pentameter is simply a line of verse containing five 'feet', each containing two syllables (so that there are ten syllables in total). For example:

'If music be the food of love, play on'

(this is the opening line of *Twelfth Night*). An **iambus** is the name given to a verse 'foot' which contains an unstressed syllable followed by a stressed syllable, as in the example:

'If **mu**/sic **be**/ the **food**/ of **love**/, play **on**'.

The iambic metre most closely reflects the rhythms of ordinary English speech. Shakespeare's iambic pentameters usually do not rhyme although he commonly uses a rhyme to indicate the end of a scene or to communicate a memorable series of thoughts. This is the metre that underlies the verse in all of Shakespeare's plays; however, in order to allow for variation in the speaking of the lines there are frequently subtle shifts in the pattern to ensure that the language does not become monotonous.

A more important aspect of the language of Shakespeare's plays than the technical points described above is that it is *poetic*. Shakespeare's verse is loaded with imagery which communicates to the audience suggestions and ideas beyond the obvious literal meanings of the words and greatly enhances the experience of watching his plays. The poetic nature of Shakespeare's expression, for example, compensates for the lack of special effects in the theatre – there was no artificial lighting but a line such as 'But soft! What light through yonder window breaks?' (from *Romeo and Juliet*) would have been sufficient to communicate to his audience that dawn was breaking.

Another technique which is a significant feature of Shakespeare's dramatic writing is his use of **soliloquies**. These are speeches in which a character in a play communicates his or her thoughts directly to the audience without other characters on stage being aware of what is said. Soliloquies are one of the key ways in which Shakespeare gives psychological depth to his characters.

Why Shakespeare is still relevant today

Shakespeare's great contemporary Ben Jonson, another dramatist, wrote that his friend and rival 'was not of an age, but for all time' and over the centuries Jonson's judgement has proved true. What makes Shakespeare so great a writer and so relevant to audiences of all periods is a combination of the force of his poetry, his technical skill as a writer for the theatre, the wealth and variety of the true-to-life characters he created and the universality of the themes of his plays. Most powerful of all, however, is the unique experience to be gained from seeing his plays in performance. It is likely that you will first become acquainted with them by reading a text in the classroom, so at all times as you read, try to imagine how the different scenes work in performance. Then, whenever possible, try to see as many live performances or film or television versions of the play you have studied as you can to appreciate fully the 'infinite variety' to be gained from the works of this great writer.

An example of Shakespeare's dramatic writing

Here is an extract from one of Shakespeare's plays for you to enjoy and to test your understanding. It is taken from *Romeo and Juliet*, a play set in Verona in Italy. Two of the leading families of the city, the Montagues and the Capulets, have been engaged in a bitter feud for generations. In this scene, Romeo, a Montague, has gone with his friend Benvolio to a masked ball at the Capulet house. He is recognised by Tybalt, one of the Capulet family, who is outraged that a Montague should have gatecrashed this party and informs Old Capulet, the head of the family, of this. Romeo, who does not realise that he has been recognised, is preoccupied with the beauty of Juliet, whom he sees for the first time. He is not aware that she is Capulet's daughter, and he approaches her to declare his love for her.

Read the scene carefully and then answer the questions that follow on page 107. Some words printed in italics have been explained for you to the right of the text.

Romeo and Juliet

Romeo:	[*To a Servingman*] What lady is that, which doth enrich the hand Of yonder knight?
Servant:	I know not, sir.
Romeo:	O, she doth teach the torches to burn bright! It seems she hangs upon the cheek of night Like a rich jewel in an Ethiope's ear; Beauty too rich for use, for earth too dear! So shows a snowy dove trooping with crows, As yonder lady o'er her fellows shows. The measure done, I'll watch her place of stand, And, touching hers, make blessed my rude hand. Did my heart love till now? forswear it, sight! For I ne'er saw true beauty till this night.
Tybalt:	This, by his voice, should be a Montague. Fetch me my rapier, boy. What dares the slave Come hither, cover'd with an antic face, To fleer and scorn at our solemnity? Now, by the stock and honour of my kin, To strike him dead, I hold it not a sin.
Capulet:	Why, how now, kinsman! wherefore storm you so?
Tybalt:	Uncle, this is a Montague, our foe, A villain that is hither come in spite, To scorn at our solemnity this night.
Capulet:	Young Romeo is it?
Tybalt:	'Tis he, that villain Romeo.
Capulet:	Content thee, gentle coz, let him alone; He bears him like a portly gentleman; And, to say truth, Verona brags of him To be a virtuous and well-govern'd youth: I would not for the wealth of all the town Here in my house do him disparagement: Therefore be patient, take no note of him: It is my will, the which if thou respect, Show a fair presence and put off these frowns, An ill-beseeming semblance for a feast.
Tybalt:	It fits, when such a villain is a guest: I'll not endure him.

Capulet:	He shall be endured: What, goodman boy! I say, he shall: go to; Am I the master here, or you? Go to. You'll not endure him! God shall mend my soul! You'll make a mutiny among my guests! You will set cock-a-hoop! You'll be the man!
Tybalt:	Why, uncle, 'tis a shame.

Capulet:	Go to, go to;
	You are a saucy boy: is't so, indeed?
	This trick may chance to scathe you, I know what:
	You must contrary me! Marry, 'tis time. [*To dancers
	    nearby.*]
	Well said, my hearts! You are a princox; go:
	Be quiet, or – [*To the Servants.*] More light, more light!
	    For shame!
	I'll make you quiet. [*To dancers.*] What, cheerly, my hearts!

Tybalt:	Patience perforce with wilful choler meeting Makes my flesh tremble in their different greeting. I will withdraw: but this intrusion shall Now seeming sweet convert to bitter gall. *Exit*
Romeo:	[*To* **Juliet**] If I profane with my unworthiest hand This holy shrine, the gentle fine is this: My lips, two blushing pilgrims, ready stand To smooth that rough touch with a tender kiss.
Juliet:	Good pilgrim, you do wrong your hand too much, Which mannerly devotion shows in this; For saints have hands that pilgrims' hands do touch, And palm to palm is holy *palmers'* kiss. pilgrims'
Romeo:	Have not saints lips, and holy palmers too?
Juliet:	Ay, pilgrim, lips that they must use in prayer.
Romeo:	O, then, dear saint, let lips do what hands do; They pray, grant thou, lest faith turn to despair.
Juliet:	Saints do not move, though grant for prayers' sake.
Romeo:	Then move not, while my prayer's effect I take. Thus from my lips, by yours, my sin is purged.
Juliet:	Then have my lips the sin that they have took.
Romeo:	Sin from thy lips? O trespass sweetly urged! Give me my sin again.
Juliet:	You kiss by the book.

Romeo and Juliet meet.

Nurse:	Madam, your mother craves a word with you.
Romeo:	What is her mother?
Nurse:	Marry, bachelor, Her mother is the lady of the house, And a good lady, and a wise and virtuous I nursed her daughter, that you talk'd withal; I tell you, he that can lay hold of her Shall have the *chinks*. money
Romeo:	Is she a Capulet? O dear account! my life is my foe's debt.
Benvolio:	Away, begone; the sport is at the best.
Romeo:	Ay, so I fear; the more is my unrest.
Capulet:	Nay, gentlemen, prepare not to be gone; We have a trifling foolish banquet towards. Is it e'en so? Why, then, I thank you all I thank you, honest gentlemen; good night. More torches here! Come on then, let's to bed. Ah, sirrah, *by my fay*, it waxes late: upon my word I'll to my rest.

Exeunt all but **Juliet** *and* **Nurse**.

Juliet:	Come hither, nurse. What is yond gentleman?
Nurse:	The son and heir of old Tiberio.
Juliet:	What's he that now is going out of door?
Nurse:	Marry, that, I think, be young Petrucio.
Juliet:	What's he that follows there, that would not dance?
Nurse:	I know not.
Juliet:	Go ask his name: if he be married. My grave is like to be my wedding bed.
Nurse:	His name is Romeo, and a Montague; The only son of your great enemy.
Juliet:	My only love sprung from my only hate! Too early seen unknown, and known too late! Prodigious birth of love it is to me, That I must love a loathed enemy.

Exercise 1: Romeo and Juliet

1 Look at Romeo's first speech, beginning 'O, she doth teach the torches …', and explain how the similes and metaphors he uses convey his impression of Juliet's beauty.

2 Imagine this scene in performance. How does Tybalt's reaction to Romeo's presence add to the tension in the scene?

3 Explain as fully as you can the difference in the behaviour of Tybalt and Old Capulet. Why do you think that Capulet behaves as he does? You should refer to the text in your answer.

4 When he first speaks to Juliet, Romeo asks if he may kiss her. Explain the metaphor in the first four lines of his speech.

5 How does Juliet respond?

6 Look closely at the dialogue between Romeo and Juliet from 'If I profane …' to '… my prayer's effect I take.' What do you notice about the form of these lines and what effect does this create?

7 What impression do you have of Juliet's nurse from what she says and does in this scene?

8 Juliet asks the Nurse, 'What is yond gentleman?' Why do you think the Nurse does not immediately refer to Romeo in her reply?

9 Explain in your own words Juliet's four lines at the end of the scene, beginning 'My only love sprung from my only hate!'

10 By referring to what people say and do throughout this scene, explain fully what you have learnt about the society of Verona, the feud between the two families, and your thoughts about the relationship between Romeo and Juliet.

Writing

1 Imagine that you are either Romeo or Juliet. After the scene in which you meet, you write your thoughts about the evening in your diary. Write your account; you do not have to try to write in Shakespearean English.
2 Write a story about a time when loyalty to a friend led to a clash with older members of a family.

Speaking and listening

Choose either the extract from *Romeo and Juliet* on pages 104–107 or a scene from a Shakespeare play that you have studied. Turn the scene into modern English then in a small group, perform your version of the scene to the rest of your class.

What happens next

Checkpoint tests your attainment in reading and writing. The questions in the actual test are likely to require you to show understanding of factual details from a passage that you are given to read (especially in Paper 1), to demonstrate your ability to interpret information and to show an appreciation of writers' techniques (especially in Paper 2). You will also be required to write a summary of information contained in one of the reading passages and to produce your own piece of informative writing for Paper 1 and some imaginative/descriptive writing for Paper 2.

If you have worked steadily through the exercises contained in *Student's Books 1–3*, you will be fully prepared for the challenge of the Checkpoint Tests. In *Student's Book 3*, for example, the exercises in Chapter 2 will have helped to prepare you for the range and type of questions contained in Checkpoint Paper 1 while Chapter 6 will have helped to prepare you for Paper 2, particularly for thinking about how writers create tension and develop a narrative. There is, therefore, no reason to fear taking the tests – rather, you should be

in a position to enjoy them and show how skilled you are in using and understanding the English language.

The skills you have acquired so far will also have provided you with a secure foundation to continue to the next phase of the Cambridge Assessment Programme, which is the two-year course leading to the International General Certificate of Secondary Education (IGCSE®) in English as a First Language, and possibly in English Literature as well.

Index